Unwritten HR Rules

21 Secrets For Attaining Awesome Career Success In Human Resources

Alan Collins

Success in HR Publishing
Chicago, Illinois USA

Dedicated to my son, Bryan.

Fifty percent of the proceeds of this book will
go to the Bryan A. Collins Memorial Scholarship Program
which provides scholarships to deserving, high potential
minority students who excel in academics and in
service to others. I encourage you to join me in
supporting this truly worthwhile cause at
www.BryanCollinsScholarship.org.

CONTENTS

Introduction – What This Book Is All About   1

Part One: No BS, Kick-Butt HR Secrets
You Can't Count On Your Boss To Tell You About

1:   *Secret #1:* The Awful, Unpleasant Truth About   8
Advancing Your Career In HR

2:   *Secret #2:* Why You Should Embrace the F-Word   16
& Use It Regularly

3:   *Secret #3:* The Real Secret To Impressing Your   21
Business Leaders

4:   *Secret #4:* How To Make More Money Faster In HR   28

5:   *Secret #5:* Go Small To Grow Big - Becoming A   37
"Tiger" In HR

6:   *Secret #6:* How To Ace Your Next HR Performance   46
Review

7:   *Secret #7:* What To Do When You Mess Up In HR   53

8:   *Secret #8:* A Simple 5-Minute Career Investment   59
You Should Make Each Week

9:   *Secret #9:* 15 Sneaky Little Ways To Take Your   66
HR Career To The Next Level Using The World's
Most Powerful Career Management Tool

Part Two: How To Attract The Best HR Career
Opportunities To Your Doorstep

10:   *Secret #10:* The P.O.W.E.R. Formula For Making   75
The Best HR Jobs Come To You

CONTENTS

11: *Secret #11:* Speak Out On Your HR Specialty 79

12: *Secret #12:* Leading & Not Waiting On Direction 87

13: *Secret #13:* Writing Proactively To Advance Your 92
  HR Career

14: *Secret #14:* How Aspiring HR Executives Use 98
  Everyday Meetings

15: *Secret #15:* The Awesome Power of Representing 104
  Your Company Externally

Part Three: Engaging Other People Who Will Help You Advance Your HR Career

16: *Secret #16:* Creating Your G.R.A.N.D. Network Of 112
  Relationships

17: *Secret #17:* HR Career Godfathers: What They Do 115
  & How They Work

18: *Secret #18:* Two People You Must Always Keep 122
  On Speed Dial

19: *Secret #19:* Utilizing Advisors & Mentors To Take 129
  Your HR Career To The Next Level

20: *Secret #20:* Networking Strategies Just For HR 139
  Professionals

21: *Secret #21:* Leveraging The Most Influential Person 152
  In Your HR Career

22: ***SPECIAL BONUS SECRET #22:*** 159
  The Most Important Unwritten HR Rule Of All

CONTENTS

A Final Word Looking Forward   173

Summary List of Unwritten HR Rules   175

Bryan A. Collins Scholarship Program   180

About the Author   181

WHAT THIS BOOK IS ALL ABOUT

As you can tell from the audacious title, this will be different than any other HR book you've ever read.

Most Human Resources books are written for HR executives. Or they focus on hot HR issues like recruitment, retaining top talent or HR metrics. And, as an aspiring HR executive, it's important for you to have books like this in your personal library. I know I do.

However, you need another type of HR book as well. You need an operating manual for managing your HR career. In *Unwritten HR Rules,* you now have this in your hands. Within these pages, you're going to find blunt, no BS, un-sugarcoated, street-smart strategies for advancing your career, impact and income in HR.

Are You Prepared To Accept The Hard Cold Realities
of Advancing Your HR Career?

Let's face it. If you want to get ahead in HR, you're not going to find the road map for doing this in any college textbook or corporate HR competency model. And yes, your masters program in HR can teach you about labor relations, staffing strategies, ERISA laws, and OD approaches, but you won't learn how to navigate through tough waters that leads to the top jobs in HR.

You may have a great boss who may close the door, let their hair down and share some of this stuff with you. I am thankful to have had a few of them. But they're hard to come by. And their advice is sometimes biased because, guess what, if you're any good at all, they want to retain you even if there are greener pastures elsewhere.

Headhunters often have their own agendas as well. They'd love a big commission check from placing you at another firm, and may not be all that interested in helping you climb the ladder where you already are.

So if you're an up and coming HR professional aspiring to the C-suite someday, and you want untainted, objective career advice, there are very few places to turn.

If any of this resonates with you, then this book is for you. It doesn't matter if you're a very seasoned HR generalist, an HR specialist, just passing through the HR function or launching your career right out of school, you'll find this book useful.

It will be especially helpful if your HR career seems stuck in a rut or you've concluded that no matter what you do, no matter how hard you work, you're not getting the appreciation, advancement opportunities or rewards you want.

As a former vice president of human resources at Pepsi, with 25 years of HR experience, I've watched some of the best HR professionals on earth get disappointed, derailed and rejected at key junctures in their HR career simply because they were unable to decipher the unwritten code of career advancement in their organizations. And no one had the guts to tell them the truth.

Lots of Folks Get Pissed With The Politics, Gamesmanship And Other Realities Which Are Simply Facts Of Life In Corporate America

This is true no matter where you work. But this can be especially true in Human Resources where the guidelines that determine who gets promoted (and who doesn't) aren't always clear cut. If you've experienced this, as I have, I can tell you that the only way to win is to know the landscape and master the rules of the game.

This book will help you address these realities and accelerate your journey towards attaining awesome success in Human Resources. It's not easy to move your career forward in the HR world. In most organizations, the HR department is the function that employees and managers love to hate. And the HR career path is not black and white. Instead, it's gray, subjective, with many different paths to the top.

You frequently work across functions and help differing groups that are at war try to find common ground. And that can create enemies. For example, when you act as a business partner, many employees think you're simply a stooge for management. When you act as an employee advocate, your managers often feel you're an annoying do-gooder. Some days, you can feel like a double agent trapped in the middle of this crossfire with no way to win in sight. Sound familiar?

I've experienced this first hand...the good, the bad and the ugly. I launched my career as a trainee in an HR rotational program at a well-known steel company and since that time, I've advanced through 16 different HR jobs in my career. I ultimately became vice president of human resources, first at Quaker Oats then at PepsiCo. In these executive roles, I've had a variety of great experiences -- including leading an organization of 60 HR directors and managers and helping them succeed; being accountable for the HR strategy for a workforce of 7000 employees across North America; serving as the mergers HR lead during both business acquisitions and divestitures; and providing HR leadership for the largest single change initiative in the history of the organization. And I've been on both sides of the aisle...having been an HR generalist, then a specialist in organization development and then a generalist again.

Now that I've left my HR executive career in corporate America and am pursuing my dream of becoming an author, I'm not bound by "political correctness." So, I don't have to sugarcoat any messages or conceal the realities of what it takes to advance in HR. I can and will tell you like it is. And that's one reason why I decided to write this book.

However, there's another reason too.

As I look back, I'm proud of the career I've had in HR. When I left Pepsi, I knew I wanted to spend the rest of my life giving back and making a difference. I frankly didn't know exactly what I would do. But I knew I wanted to continue to serve the Human Resources profession, contribute to causes that I care deeply about and continue to use my strengths to strengthen others.

I felt then and feel now obligated to do this because of the very rewarding life I've had in corporate America and because it's now time to give back. HR is such an all-consuming endeavor. More often than not in HR, your time is not your own. It is owned by the business leaders, employees, colleagues you are privileged to serve and is often spent in meetings, private discussions, coaching, traveling, meeting deadlines....and you do it over and over again. So, there isn't enough time to contribute as much as you'd like to the profession.

But now I've run out of excuses. As President Obama would say, "YOUR time has come." And he's right. This book is my way of giving back to the profession that has given me so much.

Let Me Prepare You In Advance With Some Warnings, Cautions & Confessions About This Book

This is a personal book, me talking straight with you, as if I were coaching you and as if we were sitting around in my condo looking out over the Chicago River, watching the tour boats cruise by, enjoying adult beverages and just hanging out.

Because it is personal, I'll be sharing real stories about me and my career in HR -- the good and not so good. These will be lessons learned from bare-knuckled experiences in working with business clients who are pressured every day to meet unforgiving targets for profitability, productivity, sales and costs.

I'll also be including stories and insights I've picked up from my network of exceptionally successful HR leaders and colleagues that I've been fortunate to have had at Pepsi, Quaker Oats, Gatorade, Tropicana, and Frito-Lay.

Having said all that, let me make a confession. In person, I'm naturally an even-tempered, laid-back kind of guy. The downside of that style is that I can sometimes be too subtle and

4

nuanced in my communications and sometimes people miss the point I'm trying to make. So I'm flexing my style quite a bit in this book and as you can probably tell so far, this will be a lot more too-the-point, direct, blunt and uncensored. I'm doing this because I don't want any of the essential points to be over-looked.

Also, Let Me Be Clear, You're Not Going To Find Any Consulting Theory Here

No complex business models. No change management dia-grams. No BS. No blowing smoke. Nothing pulled from 3-inch thick power point decks. None of that junk.

Instead, this book has been developed to provide you with one thing and one thing only: practical wisdom you can use right now. To do this, I've kept the chapters brief and the lessons jar-gon-free. The HR professionals that I've worked with battle time vampires all the time, struggle with work life balance and barely have time to read their emails. So I certainly wouldn't expect them to pour through some sort of 500-page research book loaded with complex diagrams, bar graphs and formulas. This book has been written to enable to you to put what you're read-ing into action immediately.

A few final cautions before you get started.

Some of this you've heard before.

Some you haven't.

Some of this you'll agree with.

Some you won't.

Some of this is going to get you mad, upset and bug the crap out of you.

Some will inspire you.

Whatever reaction you have to what I have to say, let me tell you this: If you want sugar-coated, worthless Human Resources jargon that sounds good, goes down easy but doesn't work — do us both a favor and look for it elsewhere.

You won't find it here.

However, if you want to give yourself a quantum edge in your HR career, enhance your impact, and build your income from your HR expertise (or you just need a kick in the butt to get going), buckle up, getcha' popcorn ready…and prepare to enjoy the journey that's coming up.

Best regards,

Alan Collins

Alan Collins

Part One

NO BS, KICK-BUTT HR SECRETS YOU CAN'T COUNT ON YOUR BOSS TO TELL YOU ABOUT

1

THE AWFUL, UNPLEASANT TRUTH
ABOUT ADVANCING YOUR
CAREER IN HR

I was passed over three times in two years for promotions that should have been mine.

At first, I couldn't understand why.

This all began when I landed my first real HR job at Inland Steel. I was fresh out of Purdue's masters program in industrial relations. Inland had recruited me aggressively and hired me into their well-known, fast-track Human Resources rotational program. And man, was I excited. Only one person is brought into this highly-select, prestigious program each year and I was fortunate enough to be the one selected. Inland told me that their objective was to groom me for an executive HR position in five to seven years.

Or so I thought.

The first few years I got stellar performance reviews, worked long hours, kept my nose clean and was careful not to step on anyone's toes.

I also made a couple of good lateral moves - one into labor relations, another into organization development. However, the promotions I eagerly looked forward to never happened. And from what I could tell, they weren't coming anytime soon. It didn't seem like I was on anyone's radar screen. Not only did I not get promoted, no one even took the time to call me up and tell me why. I had to do the calling myself. Clearly, from my vantage point, the organization was not showing me the love I thought I deserved.

After being passed over the first couple of times, the feedback I got was vague and unsatisfying, and I was told to hang in there. The higher ups reiterated that I was a "hand-picked, high flyer" and that "my time was coming soon." So I waited.

A few months later, I was blindsided and passed over for yet a third time. No courtesy phone call. No advanced notice. No communications. Nothing.

And this time, I just lost it!

I was crushed and dumbfounded and had a lot of sleepless nights as I struggled with what to do or say. For days, I mentally wrestled with a number of questions: Is putting in all these long hours and busting my butt to complete projects on time really worth it? Does getting good feedback on your work not count? Was I being passed over because I was black? Is my style a problem because I'm a bit more laid back and not an "in-your-face" HR type? Frankly, I didn't know whether to quit or stay.

Finally, I decided to arrange some sit-downs and get some answers from the key decision makers. My boss seemed clueless, so I went over his head. I didn't want to do that, but I felt I had no choice.

When I met with the higher ups, I didn't pull any punches. And they didn't either! And because they were brutally candid with me, this turned out to be the best thing that ever happened. In fact, what they gave me was...

The Single Best Piece Of Advice I Ever Got In My HR Career!

It was a wake-up call. What they told me wasn't anything new. I'd heard it lots of times before. But I didn't realize until that moment how truly important it really was. Or maybe after being passed over, I was now ready to finally "hear" their feedback.

In any event, I've now come to call their advice the awful, unpleasant truth about advancing your career in HR. It is simply this...

You Don't Get Promoted In HR, Unless You Promote Yourself.

Even though this happened many years back, I remember just about every word that was said. It went something like this...

"Alan, success in HR is not only about working harder and putting in more hours than everybody else. You're already doing that. It's also about how to position yourself and make yourself and your accomplishments more visible in the organization."

"Now don't mistake what we're saying, there's nothing wrong with doing your job. We'll fire you if you don't."

But, just doing your job well, even exceptionally well, just doesn't cut it if you want to advance your career to the highest levels."

"What does work is making sure that you actively promote yourself and your work. Unless your boss knows you're exceptional - and so does his boss - and anyone else who could be your next boss, you might as well be invisible. And you have absolutely no shot at advancing your career."

"Working hard and expecting that your results alone will be recognized, noticed, or rewarded with promotions guarantees one thing and one thing only: old age. And focusing on doing what you do better than anyone else and trusting that that alone is enough, also guarantees you one thing and one thing only: a long life laboring in oblivion."

After Listening To This, I Felt Like I Had Been Punched In The Gut.

But I got the message. As much as this hurt to hear, this was great advice.

Apparently, while my boss gave me great reviews, he wasn't doing much to talk up my readiness to assume larger HR roles. So, when open positions became available, I had no one advocating on my behalf with the key decision-makers. And I certainly didn't think it was my job to do this, I thought my results would speak for themselves.

I now knew this was naïve and I had made a big mistake.

And, it was now time for me to accept this reality and do something with it. So, after a lot of soul-searching, I concluded that it was too late to make up for five years of lost time at Inland and this boss, and I left.

I joined Quaker Oats...but not before fully embracing this blunt, unpleasant truth. I didn't want to make this mistake again.

And I didn't.

The minute I committed myself to taking charge, becoming more visible and owning the accountability for promoting my own accomplishments was the moment my career turned around for the better.

Yes, I got the message. And from this very painful first experience in HR, I learned my first set of unwritten HR rules about career advancement:

#1: To succeed in HR, great ability is not enough, you also need great visibility. You can't assume that the key decision-makers automatically know what you're contributing. I don't care if you're in an entry level HR position doing grunt work or in an executive VP HR role setting the people strategy for an entire organization. This unpleasant truth is the same. If you think that the key decisions makers are always in the loop about what you're doing and how you're adding value, you're wrong. Most are too consumed with their own work and thinking about themselves to worry about you. Like you, they're trying to avoid getting trampled to death in a world that seems to get bigger, noisier, more competitive and faster each week. So, you have to cut through this clutter. To do this, it's your responsibility to make sure they know what you're contributing by promoting yourself, staying visible and getting the word out about how you're adding value to the organization. Flying under the radar may be good for geese, but it's a terrible strategy if you want to advance your career.

#2: Managing your HR career is not the same thing as doing your HR job. *They are separate processes.* You can be the most competent HR professional in your organization and at the same time be neglecting or even destroying your career. On the other hand, if you spend more time managing your HR career than doing your job, you will fail too. *So, you need to do both.* No matter what your boss or your favorite headhunter says, no one else owns your career except you. This means that the absolute worst thing you can possibly do is to bury your head in "day to day HR grunt work," and not take enough time to make yourself visible.

#3: You must engage in relentless, continuous, uninterrupted, constant self-promotion in order to keep your HR career moving forward. The key words here are "relentless," "continuous," "uninterrupted" and "constant." Like many of us, I was taught at an early age that modesty is a virtue. I was told that all you need to do is to keep your head down, work hard and you'll get rewarded. This advice though well-meaning, is misguided. Just to be noticed and respected, you'll need to get comfortable beating your chest, pounding your own drum and tooting your own horn. *But, doing it in the right way.*

The problem is that most HR folks view themselves as "doers" of what they do, with the tasks of marketing themselves and their accomplishments regarded as a necessary evil. However, I contend that those that "market" themselves are much more valuable and more highly paid than doers.

This doesn't only apply to generalists, but to HR specialists too. When the recruiting specialist starts promoting her staffing services, or the compensation manager in HR starts marketing his team's comp services, or the labor relations VP sells her labor negotiations expertise inside the organization, each of these different people take a quantum leap up in income potential.

#4: To successfully toot your own horn, you must know how to do it in subtle ways. You can't market yourself by coming across as some kind of glory-hound, braggart or conceited, obnoxious jerk. Or your colleagues will despise you and your HR career is dead before you get out of the starting gate. But on the other hand, if you don't tell people about your accomplishments, no one else will. So, what do you do? The rest of this book provides tons of strategies for addressing this question, but let me give you a few pieces just to chew on right now...

- **Provide updates, instead of bragging.** Make sure you set up frequent (at least twice monthly) opportunities to showcase your accomplishments by providing simple "updates" or "progress reports" to your boss and the key decision-makers. Everyone wants to know what's going on, especially in large organizations. So filling this information void with status updates on your work is not viewed as offensive. It's viewed as positive and helpful. For example, you might say in one of these update sessions: *"We've achieved an important goal in the union labor negotiations by tentatively agreeing to contract out 20% of all maintenance work, which is valued at $2 million. We are pleased that our discussions are proceeding along according to our timetable. Should things continue as they have been going, we should conclude negotiations in the next three days, which will be one week ahead of schedule..."*

- **Use a "we-first," not a "me-first" approach.** When talking about your accomplishments to others, make your message "we" instead of "me." Emphasize how what you've done has benefitted your colleagues and the company as a whole. For example in an e-mail to your boss or your client, you might say: *"Thought you'd like to know that our team has just completed the new restructuring plan in the Finance Department and reduced headcount by 9%. With great job evaluation and com-*

pensation information supplied by Karen and Heather, and the support of the Finance Leadership team, we were able to..."

- **Utilize P.O.W.E.R. strategies.** These strategies are shrewd and subtle but can provide a quantum leap to your visibility and elevate you to HR rock star status, if done well. They are laid out in Chapters 10-15. You will want to consult these techniques often.

- **Surround yourself with a G.R.A.N.D. team that can help promote you and your career**. As I learned from this first excruciating, yet growthful experience, my boss was doing nothing to promote my career. It's important that you have your boss in your corner, but it's more important to have an entire team working on your behalf. In Chapters 16-21, you can read about the G.R.A.N.D. team you should put in place to help you market your career and your accomplishments.

So, let me wrap up this first chapter by saying this: I believe the most important decision you'll ever make in your HR career is the decision to start selling yourself. When that happens, I predict that day will mark the point that your HR career turns around for the better.

In reality, you really only have two choices. You can choose to stick up your nose at the HR folks who are self-promoters, criticize them and criticize the practice of self-promotion yourself, view it as unseemly, as beneath you, as crass, and stand around complaining about it. OR you can get good at it yourself and use it to create influence, prominence, prestige, credibility, career and financial success in HR.

The choice is yours.

Unwritten HR Rule #1:

You don't get promoted in HR, unless you promote yourself. To succeed in HR, great ability is not enough, you need great visibility.

"Flying under the radar may be good for geese, but it's a terrible strategy if you want to advance your HR career."

2

WHY YOU SHOULD EMBRACE THE F-WORD & USE IT REGULARLY

Relax, this F-word is not what you think! F is for feedback.

Sometimes the reason you're not making the career progress you want is because you're absolutely clueless about the buzz about you. Or you have, in fact, received some feedback, but it's vague, fuzzy and you're uncertain what it really means.

A few years back, I overheard a conversation taking place in the office next door by an HR executive I knew in another division of Pepsi. Given that the walls were paper thin, and not well insulated, it was easy to make out what was being said.

The person he talking to was Rick, one of his direct reports, about 30 years old, who used this meeting to dump out a load of unhappiness and frustration. Rick complained that he was underpaid. The organization sucked. His clients weren't paying enough attention to him. No one returned his calls. His HR counterparts at corporate, who he had to work with on projects, were always tied up and never available for meetings.

Finally, after listening to this whining long enough, the HR executive jumped in and said: "I hear you. We've all been there. Rick, have you asked your clients and colleagues for any feedback? Have you asked them about their major priorities and what you can do to help them? "

"No, they're always too busy. And like I said, I never get my calls returned. This is completely unacceptable." was the reply.

He was right, it was unacceptable. For *him.*

One month later Rick was fired!

All he did was complain, grouse and makes excuses about why things couldn't get done. Sometimes the problem was an HR policy that stood in the way. Other times he said compensation guidelines or potential lawsuits were hurdles, even though his HR peers had found pockets of flexibility within these same guidelines. Still other times, he simply flat out failed to follow through on what he promised.

Finally, his clients and colleagues were fed up. After telling Rick repeatedly that he needed to show more "thought leadership," more "innovation," and be more of a "proactive entrepreneur" in his work, they gave up and went to his boss and complained that they couldn't work with him. And his boss, not known for his patience, acted quickly by putting him first on a performance improvement plan and then dumping him one month later.

The sad thing is that at his termination meeting, Rick was dumbfounded. He never saw the ax coming. Sure, he owned up to having received feedback but said he had no clue what "thought leadership" was or what being more "entrepreneurial" meant. He thought this information was much too vague, mysterious and imprecise for him to act on.

So he ignored these important cues.

Unfortunately, his failure to dig deeper and decipher the real message lurking beneath the surface of these "labels" and "code words" wound up costing him his job.

Rick's situation is surprisingly common, especially among HR professionals not versed in the unwritten rules about how most organizations work. *Very few organizations give feedback well.* It is often unclear and confusing...sometimes intentionally so...because it's uncomfortable to provide it and because no one wants to chase away good performers. So, it's up to you to get beyond the labels and cryptic statements – to dig out the *real* concerns about how you're viewed in the organization.

Do you know what the HR community in your organization is saying about you? Your clients? Your boss? If not, you're missing the boat. You need this feedback, especially if it's bad. And, you need it even if it's vague, doesn't make sense, inconsistent or even unfair. Without it, you are overlooking important perspectives that will hold back your career.

Getting feedback can be a very intimidating task for a lot of people. Our ego gets in the way. It's never easy hearing criticism, and this is what many people fear. However, the only way to enhance your HR career is to get this kind of feedback and act on it.

Here's Are Actions You Should Take Now
To Utilize The F-word:

Set up time to get face-to-face feedback immediately. If you regularly get 360 feedback reports, that's great...*but it's not enough.* You should be prepared to go beyond these reports to dive into the real issues through face-to-face dialog. Pick out a small collection of people who know you, work with you and who will be candid. This could be peers, your boss, or your clients. Do this in person, not by email. Face-to-face allows it to become more of a two-way dialog and fluid question and answer session. Once they agree, set up a meeting time in a private, closed door room.

Of course, the possibility exists that they may not be straight with you or their perspectives may differ from those of the most senior HR decision-makers. So, for additional validation, you might have conversations with your former manager or your boss' boss. Try to contact the highest level manager who is knowledgeable about your work, and with whom you have a good relationship so your approach seems natural and appropriate. However, don't go around your boss. He or she should know about any contact you have with other executives and what your intentions are.

Write down and be prepared to accept as accurate everything you hear. At the meeting, be sure to jot down everything they suggest. Getting past the reluctance to provide direct and difficult feedback can be challenging for the people providing it. So it is important that you show a sincere desire to hear their perspectives – and resist the urge to be argumentative. This is not a personal attack on you. So, get into active listening mode. Any comment you make or non-verbal cue you give off that conveys defensiveness will either shut down the flow of feedback or steer it to safer (and much vaguer) code-word territory...such as the "be more entrepreneurial" comments that Rick heard. You don't have to agree with everything. And, if you don't agree with something, ask clarifying questions, but don't debate. (You can always go back and correct the facts later; but this isn't the time). The worst thing you can say in one of these sessions is: "I disagree with that." The feedback you're getting is a gift – of time, honesty and thoughtful insight. And, as a gift, the best response to any feedback – good or bad, whether you agree with it or not – is "thank you."

If you're having trouble decoding the feedback you receive, probe deeper. Some feedback you'll hear can be especially hard to nail down because it often doesn't pertain to your specific HR skills and experience. Instead, it relates to the "softer" aspects of your style in leading, communicating and working with others. Being told you're "too abrasive," "too laid back," "too serious" or "uncommitted" are examples of feedback that isn't actionable. So, when you hear these types of statements, ask: "What one or two things – beyond anything else – would you recommend that I do that would help me address this and be more effective?" As long as the other person is candid and truthful, this question will significantly help clarify unclear and puzzling comments.

Act on what you've learned and let your feedback providers know you're acting on it. From clients, for example, you may find themes in their answers such as: "It takes too long to for you to call me back…" or "You do a great job of identifying issues within our team, but you don't spend enough time bringing forward solutions to help…" In response, let your clients know that you've heard them and share what improvements you are making as a result of their feedback. This will help build your relationship with them and also make it much more comfortable for them to provide helpful feedback in the future.

Whether you decide to actively solicit feedback or not, keep your antenna out for feedback that might find you. Remember Rick's story. Nobody likes a complainer and tough times give managers free rein to get rid of people who make their lives a living hell. So, stay optimistic, flexible, and ready to clarify, probe and de-code any unexpected, off-the-cuff comments you hear related to your performance and your career advancement opportunities.

Unwritten HR Rule #2

Embrace and use the F-word regularly. Set up regular face-to-face meetings to clarify, dig deeper and de-code any vague and confusing feedback you receive. Consider feedback a gift and when receiving it, the most appropriate response is: "Thank you!"

"In HR as in life, your supporters make you happy but it's your critics that make you better"

3

THE REAL SECRET TO IMPRESSING YOUR BUSINESS LEADERS

As an aspiring HR executive, you absolutely must have the ability to gain credibility and work successfully with senior business leaders.

Sadly, many HR folks continue to complain about how tough it is to be taken seriously and win a seat at the leadership table where the big boys and girls sit. I can't tell you how many discussions I've had in the past with my HR colleagues where much of the time was spent on questions like: "Why can't I get any respect?" "Why is my opinion not being sought out?" or "I feel like a neglected step-child, why am I not being treated as a full member of the team?"

Even well-read, popular articles like "Why We Hate HR" (*Fast Company*) and "Memo To CFOs: Don't Trust HR" (*CFO Magazine*) have picked up on this theme. These articles have spread the perspective, held by many, that most HR people spend too much time on administrivia, lack credibility within their organizations and are not impact players in contributing to the success of their businesses.

Here's my candid take on all this: Deal with it or change!

If you're in HR and you're not helping to drive the business forward, you deserve being treated like a second class citizen.

You don't deserve a seat at the table and all the articles disparaging HR are warranted and they apply to you.

But, on the other hand, if you want to change this perception and join the breed of HR people that are in huge demand by business leaders...the type of person readily invited to share their HR experience and expertise in critical business situations...then it starts with embracing the secret the best HR people know. And that secret is this...

It's Easy To Impress Your Business Leaders As An HR Professional...*When You've Impressed Them With Your Knowledge Of Their Business First!*

Anyone that has become off-the-charts successful in HR does so by first getting brilliant on their business. I don't mean the HR business. But the business that is providing you with a paycheck. Succeeding in HR requires high degrees of influence and personal persuasion with business leaders. And that only comes by knowing your business well enough that you can tie your HR programs and initiatives to the business and leverage them to move that business forward.

Here's a quick test: Let's say, you're an HR manager in the Gatorade business at Pepsi, and your Gatorade general manager was out sick, could you step in and give his 30 minute monthly financial update to the leadership team? Could you describe the current challenges facing the business? Or talk with confidence about how Gatorade is made, where it's made, how it makes money, and how the product has been positioned to attract consumers in the marketplace? And could you describe the P&L impact of the HR programs and initiatives you're accountable for. Tough standard? Yes. Impossible? Definitely not. The top HR people can pass tests like these for their businesses with flying colors.

At Pepsi, we called this ability "knowing the business cold" and all of our very best HR people, the ones that were true partners with their business leaders, had this skill in spades. And, you'd be amazed at the credibility they had, how much they were valued and how well they were able to impact the performance their business.

Knowing the business cold is one of the qualities that differentiate Pepsi HR leaders from the rest of the pack. In fact, according to *HR Executive*, Pepsi has produced more Chief HR officers in Fortune 1000 organizations than any other company on earth.

Want to know how you can join this group? Here's what it takes:

Align your HR initiatives tightly to your business priorities and minimize the church work. A Pepsi executive I worked with often referred to many HR initiatives as "church work." These were HR programs he felt were primarily geared to make people happy, had questionable value and were implemented whether or not they helped move the business forward.

To confess, I've done my share of church work. One of the stupidest mistakes, I ever made was trying to sell our business leaders on piloting a flextime program in a tiny business within our company. There was nothing wrong with this except that I did it during a terrible financial year and without knowing this particular business was up for sale! This business was bleeding cash, needed all hands on deck and it was crucial that we get rid of it. However, I only looked at our culture survey results for this business which indicated that this was our #1 people issue. It was a nice idea. But the timing was wrong. It was not aligned to the strategy of this business. It was HR for HR sake. Church work. And dumb.

You should avoid being a part of initiatives like this at all costs.

Get off your duff and build your business acumen. It's a fallacy to think that staying in your office and doing paperwork and email will help you learn your business. As a junior HR generalist, I was told: "You need to get out and walk the plant floor on regular basis. That's the best way of getting a pulse beat on the business. In fact, if you don't have to buy a pair of shoes every six months, you're not doing your job." I was working at Inland's steel manufacturing plant at the time and this was great advice. And this is just as applicable if you're in HR at head-quarters, a sales office or in a non-profit organization.

Here are some additional ways of building your business acumen:

- Enlist the help of an advisor or coach who has deep financial, sales and business expertise to work with you.
- Set up sessions with your Finance Department. Spend time observing and maybe even assisting the accounts payable clerks in paying the bills.
- Arrange to spend some time in your purchasing group. Observe and roll up your sleeves and offer to help the purchasing clerks order goods or services.
- Set aside a few hours on a regular basis and stand by and watch how the customer service rep works with irate customer calls.
- Get some of your sales reps to let you go on sales calls with them to learn the needs of the customers and consumers of your business.
- If your company has manufacturing plants, get out in the field with folks on the frontline on a regular basis. Walk the plant floor and talk to the employees making the product every chance you get.
- Whenever possible, set up routine meetings with others on their turf (not yours) to learn the challenges they face in their area of the organization.
- Start a regular reading program on your business. This includes: Arranging to get copied on internal monthly and quarterly financial and business updates; becoming familiar with the strategic business plans for your unit; reading your company's annual report; reading the same industry trade publications or investor reports that your business leaders read; and beefing up your understanding of balance sheets and P&L statements. For the latter, Google: "How To Read A Financial Report" published by Merrill Lynch and download it online.

ATTAINING AWESOME CAREER SUCCESS IN HR

Be a business person first, an HR person second. This is an overused phrase in HR, but here's what it means: when coming to the table with the top dogs, drop the HR jargon. It is a mistake to think that speaking HR psychobabble, or giving "HR opinions" and "HR perceptions," without conveying how your idea touches the P&L, will carry much weight when trying to gain credibility with your business leaders. Many HR professionals aren't numbers people. But you should be. Speaking in numbers, not words, elevates your status. Numbers and dollars are the language of business. And to earn your seat at the table with your leadership team, you should not treat this as a foreign language.

You will not be influential with your business leaders, if you can't present numbers or fact-based arguments that will impress your CEO & CFO. Backing up your HR decisions with facts and data like ROI, payback period, and dollar impact should become second nature. For example, instead of saying "our campus recruiting program is very productive!" Talk about how the recruitment program will increase "revenue per employee" or "new hire performance" (e.g. their job performance rating after 12 months) or decrease "new hire failures" (% of new hires in key jobs that were terminated or asked to leave). Numbers and dollars will provide punch and influence for your HR proposals.

Adjust your HR priorities. In some organizations, we in HR are often "too busy" to attend important business update meetings. Or we're "out of town" when early decisions are being discussed to buy a business or to layoff employees. As a result, we've lost an opportunity to impact the business and elevate our reputation because we are brought in only after these key decisions have been made. And in the process, we subtly communicate that HR priorities are more important than the business priorities.

Everyone's busy and a few absences are understood.

However, doing this on a regular basis reinforces the stereotype of HR as a function separate from the rest of the business. You want to convey that leaving you out of these discussions is a horrible mistake. And to do that, you have to adjust your priorities. Treat your role within your company as if you're one of the owners responsible for running the business. And adjust your own schedule accordingly.

Also, as you participate in these discussions, pay close attention to costs, as if it were your own money. Make people decisions as if you're paying for them out of your own pocket. In one-on-ones with your business leaders, instead of discussing the latest HR dilemma, make it point to talk up the business and give your own point of view on current customer and marketing strategies as well as ways you've thought about to enhance the performance of the business. *Regularly thinking and behaving like an owner, and talking with equal comfort about both HR and business issues, will help connect you more closely and elevate your status in the minds of your business leaders.*

Get passionate about your business or get out. Some HR folks have confided in me privately that they just can't "feel" the businesses they're working in. Try as they might, they just can't get pumped up about what the business does.

And I understand fully.

For example, if you're working for a consumer products company like Pepsi – an organization that markets and sells soda pop, bottled water, orange juice, oatmeal, and potato chips -- it's pretty easy to identify with the product because it's in your kitchen. Everyone consumes it. It's fun food. It's easy to talk about. It hits home. Getting to know this business can be fun and enjoyable.

But if you're working for a company that makes some sort of micro-electronic circuit that goes into a motherboard that then is put into some other piece of equipment, it's hard to work up some enthusiasm about this business. Also, it's very hard to describe this to others when you're at parties or family reunions. At least for me, it would be.

But this changes absolutely nothing.

The facts remain the same. You've got to be a zealous, enthusiastic advocate for your business and know it deeply or it will handicap your ability to advance in HR in your organization.

Can some HR people succeed by not knowing and being passionate about their businesses? Sure. Some people win the lottery, too! And your odds are about the same. So, if you can't "feel" the business you're in, resolve TODAY to:

(1) Find some small part of the business you're currently in that excites you, OR

(2) Transfer to a division or a different business within your company that turns you on, OR

(3) LEAVE and find a different opportunity elsewhere!

If you want to be credible with business leaders, don't ever, ever make the mistake of giving the business' priorities a backseat to those of the HR function. The only exceptions to this rule are business situations that are illegal, immoral or unethical. Otherwise, the more you approach your job like a business owner and live the business, the more credibility you'll have with your business leaders and the faster you'll position yourself to enhance your career in HR.

Unwritten HR Rule #3

It's easy to impress your business leaders as an HR professional...when you've impressed them with your knowledge of their business first!

4

HOW TO MAKE A LOT MORE
MONEY FASTER IN HR

If your HR career lasts 10 years, your total gross earnings for
that period should reach the $1 million dollar mark, *at least.* (If
it doesn't, you probably shouldn't be reading this book.) However, just how quickly you reach that mark – whether it takes
you the full 10 years, or whether you need only 5 years or just 2
years – will depend a lot on what we'll discuss in this chapter.

Let's face it, making money is important. It's not the end all,
be all. And it's more important to some HR folks than others.
But it's darn important.

I've never read an HR book that laid out a plan for making
money faster as an HR professional. Or any HR article for that
matter. So this chapter will be breaking some new ground.

Some HR folks I've talked with believe there is something
unseemly, boorish and crude about talking openly about techniques for raking in more cash in HR and doing it fast. I don't!
There is no virtue in making money slowly. And there's nothing
wrong with doing it quickly. When your paycheck is direct de-
posited in your bank, they don't add a bonus for "slow" or
deduct a penalty for "fast." And, no one will put you behind

bars based on how fast you increase you pay, unless you do it illegally, which is not the focus of the chapter.

So let's drop all these mental roadblocks and start talking about this unwritten HR rule.

The secret to making more money faster in HR is to look for ways to *add massive amounts of value* to your clients and to your organization. And then doing it!

That's it.

It's that simple.

However, before you pooh-pooh this as simply more HR-speak, my experience has been that most HR people are absolutely clueless about what adding value is really all about.

So, let me give you an example that illustrates...

What Adding Massive Value In HR
REALLY Means So You Never Have To
Settle For That Measly 2-3% Annual
Merit Increase Ever Again!

The story behind this example is true but I'm concealing names to preserve relationships. It's also somewhat lengthy, but stay with me and you'll get the point at the end. Ready? Let's begin.

Envision that you head up the talent management department at your company and you've had trouble recruiting female engineering candidates. While sipping your coffee one morning, you read in the newspaper that the Society of Women Engineers (SWE) is holding a one-day seminar that 300 of the top women engineers from all over the country are expected to attend. The conference is being held in the city's largest conference center only four blocks from your office.

You recognize instantly that this seminar is good news for your company and for your recruiting problem. Unfortunately, so does your competitor across the street, who heads up their HR department and who has the exact same recruiting dilemma. You're deliriously happy because all these women will be clustered together at one location, which gives you a great chance to recruit some of them to your company.

So, you call the SWE conference organizers and they agree that you can set up a table outside of the SWE seminar conference room during the lunch period. All your company's brochures, annual reports and flyers describing your company's employment opportunities for engineers will be available...along with a giant poster with your company's logo. For good measure, you've also arranged for two of your best female engineers to be there with you at the table to help flag down the attendees to talk about your company's career opportunities once the seminar breaks for lunch.

Nice plan? Well, not so fast.

Let's Flash Forward To The Day The Seminar Is Held To See How Well Your Plan Delivers

You arrive at 11 a.m. with your two engineering colleagues in tow and set up the table. When noon arrives you're ready.

However, when the seminar door opens at noon, the SWE attendees rush by your table and immediately board four shuttle buses outside. No one pauses to stop at your table. It doesn't take long for the busses to fill to capacity. You notice as the women are passing by your table, they're chatting up a storm and they're all holding a flyer in their hands. Quickly getting a copy of this flyer yourself, you learn that this shuttle is taking them to a "complimentary lunch and CEO presentation" at your HR competitor's company headquarters just a few blocks away!

Stunned by all of this, you decide to regroup. You and your two engineers grab a quick bite at the restaurant across the street to talk. Over lunch, you decide to stay until the end of the seminar so that the entire day isn't a wasted effort. Unfortunately, because of prior commitments, your two engineers have to leave. So you're now going back to the seminar alone.

Ninety minutes later, the SWE members return and file out of the buses all holding "goodie bags" with your competitor's logo on them. As they re-enter the meeting room, they all seem quite excited and energized about their experience at lunch. And now, because the seminar is behind schedule, the facilitators are rushing everyone back into the room to make up for lost time.

Still shaken by what has happened and now operating solo, you wait patiently outside the meeting room until the seminar concludes. When it does, the SWE attendees emerge in a rush. Many are clearly exhausted from the full day and most are ready to get home. You're only able to quickly grab and talk with a couple of them. However, because of seminar fatigue, most clearly have other things on their mind and are not prepared to engage in any kind of lengthy dialog at this point. Reading the dynamics of this situation...

You Decide To Pick Up and Head Out Recognizing You Are In No Better Situation Than You Were When the Day Started!

You think: "I don't have one single frickin' lead on a female engineering candidate." Frustrated, you go to bed that night with a sigh, knowing that the day has been a tremendous waste of time.

And this is all confirmed the next day in the morning newspaper. There's a story on the front page about your competitor with a headline that reads: "ABC Company Hosts CEO Lunch & Career Forum For Society of Women Engineers." The CEO is pictured surrounded by SWE attendees, all of whom have gleeful smiles on their faces. The story goes on to say that fifty of the SWE attendees, over the next few weeks, will return for follow up interviews at the company's expense.

As you read this your heart sinks.

You missed a golden opportunity. And now it's conclusive: your HR competitor has kicked your butt!

Having The Midas Touch For Improving Results Is What Adding Value In HR Is All About

Here's the point in this overly long example: *Having an innovative strategy alone with no results to show for it, is NOT adding value.* If you think about it, in this example, you had an innovative strategy (going onsite to the meeting, setting up your table, including two of your best female engineers), but it produced no results. This is where most HR folks are misinformed. Innovation is a nice exercise but, by itself, does not add value.

On the other hand, not only was your competitor's recruitment strategy more innovative (shuttle busses, lunch, CEO involvement), but it delivered great RESULTS too. From this one effort, he was able to get more female engineering candidate leads than you, secure more interviews than you and a few weeks from now will no doubt produce more hires than you. This is what adding value in HR is all about.

Added value in HR means IMPROVING TANGIBLE RESULTS THAT YOUR ORGANIZATION CARES ABOUT. Clearly, in this case, your HR competitor added more value for their organization and their company's recruitment effort than you did for yours.

And, coming up with ways that deliver these kinds of results on a consistent basis not only enables you to stand out, but is the pathway to making more money in HR.

As you think about this, it's important to note that...

Just Because You've Done Your HR Job For 10 Years, That Doesn't Automatically Mean That You're Worth More Or Should Be Paid More Than Someone Who's Done Theirs For 10 Months!

As an HR executive at Pepsi, I've had to tell many of my hard-working, long service HR managers the bad news that they didn't want to hear: certain jobs are only worth a certain salary...and not one penny more...no matter how long you've been doing that job.

Now, this was nothing new to my HR managers because they convey this counsel their clients all the time when responding to compensation questions. However, it's a totally different experience telling this to someone and hearing someone else say this to you.

"But I've got five years of HR experience and I'm worth more than Susan, who's only been on the job two years," they'll tell me.

Sorry, but seniority in HR jobs, by itself, does NOT entitle you to more money. The length of time a person is in a job doesn't necessarily increase the real value of getting that job done. The only thing that counts is *how much value you add* in terms of *improving the results your company cares about.*

Politicians And Especially Unions Have Perpetuated This "Seniority Myth" For Their Own Gains And Have Misled The Public On This Issue For Years!

Believe me, I understand. So, when someone asks: "How can I get more than just the same token 2-3% raise that everybody else is getting?" I reply quickly by suggesting that they go find a full-length mirror, sit down in a chair facing it, stare deeply into his or her own eyes and ask: "What am I going to do to add more value to my company and improve the results my organization cares about?" Again, the key words here are "adding value" and "results my organization cares about."

The harsh reality is if you are not delivering more of this type of value to your organization or your clients, and if you are not making yourself indispensable to them every day, then you are declining in value to them.

In most large corporations, there are entire departments of HR people doing the very same jobs, the same way year after year, and they are shocked when new technology, offshoring or some other "replacement" boots them out on the street.

Every one of these people has one distinctive attribute in common: from one year to the next they have not taken any initiative to deliver more value in their work...or to increase their own value.

Let me go even further, if someone is not telling you that what you're contributing is, in fact, advancing the business proposition of the company, you quickly create questions about whether or not you should be in that job -- or whether that job is really needed! I know by now I've beaten a dead horse on this, but I really want to drive this point home…

**To Earn More Than Just The Typical Average Merit
Increase, Simply Figure Out A Way To Give
Triple the Value You Are Giving Right Now
To Your Employer, Customers, Clients,
Boss or Colleagues!**

If you do this, I predict with absolute confidence that one of the following will happen:

1. Your present employer will respond with raises, bonuses and advancement opportunities well beyond your expectations.

2. A new employer (or one of your company's competitors) will find you, grab you, immediately recognize how you can help them and hike up your pay by a minimum of 10%, but probably more.

3. You'll discover a lucrative entrepreneurial opportunity that allows you to develop and package your skills (or the *value you add that companies care about)* in such a way that lots of organizations will beat a path to your door – hiring you as their consultant, their coach, or their trainer teaching their staffs -- and you'll move on to writing your own paycheck and being your own boss.

I firmly believe that your compensation will always catch up to your value. Maybe not right away, but in time. However, you have to be prepared to go where your value will be recognized.

**Three Steps You Can Take Now To Add More Value
And Begin The Process of Increasing Your Income Faster**

Step 1: Think first about what results your clients or your organization want most. Identify those areas where your organization is at a competitive disadvantage or results that your clients have complained about most.

- Is it improved retention?
- Is it cost savings or cutting overhead?
- Is it getting higher quality job candidates?
- Is it improving customer service?
- Is it improving the results from the sales force?
- Is it lack of talent in some regions?
- Is it changing the skill mix of the workforce?
- Is it moving work to lower cost areas of the country?
- Is it improving teamwork between two functions at war?
- Is it spreading best practices internally?
- Is it expanding the online presence of the company?
- Is it reducing overtime, tardiness or sick leave usage?

Step 2: Pick one of these outcomes, put a metric to it and then commit yourself to develop strategies to blast it out of the park. Let's say your organization's biggest priority is cost savings. Strategies you could develop and implement could include:

- Developing recruitment systems that allow managers to hire less expensive or less experienced employees for lower skilled positions.
- For manufacturing locations, providing advice and tools for reducing unnecessary overtime.
- Providing your leadership team with best practices for decreasing the cost of labor required to produce each unit of product or service your organization delivers.
- Coming up with a non-monetary incentive or recognition program for employees who help drive down costs.

It is this ability to propose – and successfully implement – value-added solutions that contribute to addressing big organization problems that truly differentiate the HR top earners from those just making a decent salary.

Step 3: Update your resume every year by documenting the value you've added over the previous calendar year. I believe doing this is more important for increasing your income longer term than any merit increases that follow your performance reviews. By simply taking time to religiously note your annual achievements on your resume, you will enhance your resume's value in the marketplace and your attractiveness to recruiters. Think about how your resume would be improved if you were to add this new entry to it at the end of the year: *"As HR director for the IT group, because of two new culture building initiatives we put in place, our culture survey results improved by 25%, IT turnover dropped from 12% to 6% and our overtime costs went down by $1.2MM or 4%."*

Now that's adding <u>real value</u>. And, when you're able to enhance your resume with this kind of achievement every year, making money faster in HR will not be a problem.

###

Extra Bonus Tip! For another example that illustrates how adding value can enable you to make more money faster in HR, check out my article: *The Employee Free Choice Act – An Unbelievable Opportunity for HR.* You can find it at: http://SuccessInHR.com/employee-free-choice-act-hr.

<u>Unwritten HR Rule #4</u>

The key to making a lot more money in HR is by adding massive value. Adding value is figuring out ways to improve results in areas your organization cares deeply about. And then doing it!

"Don't chase money. Do HR work that truly inspires other people or helps your company succeed and the money will chase you."

5

GO SMALL TO GROW BIG:
BECOMING A "TIGER" IN HR

Another strategy for taking command of your HR career and driving it forward is to go small to grow big.

Going small means you dedicate yourself to one, single area of HR and commit yourself to becoming your organization's in-house expert or it's "go-to" person for this one thing. And then you grow big by leveraging this one area into larger and more lucrative HR roles. I call this becoming a "Tiger" in HR.

Why? Because of Tiger Woods. The "good" Tiger Woods.

At one time in his career, before his high-publicized "indiscretions" and his horribly stupid downfall, no one disputed that Tiger was the top golfer in the world...*for ten consecutive years!*

And, if you look at that ten-year time span in Tiger's career, you'll notice something else. By choosing to specialize and commit to the ONE, small, single, narrow niche of golf, his career skyrocketed and grew even bigger.

He not only became the best *golfer*. He leveraged his golf reputation to build a gigantic multi-billion dollar empire that included non-profit foundations, learning centers for children, college scholarship grants, fundraising, publishing, golf course design companies, video games, TV commercials, corporate endorsements and even his own sports drink. And, in the process, he enlarged his career from being merely another golfer to one of the most marketable celebrities on the planet.

Now let's contrast what Tiger did during that time with two other sports superstars: Michael and Magic.

In 1994, Michael Jordan, despite his reputation as the world's greatest basketball player, failed when he switched careers entirely to try the game of baseball.

Four years later, Magic Johnson, the hall-of-fame basketball star, failed trying a new career as a late night TV talk show host.

In both cases, Michael and Magic experienced shocking career setbacks by failing to play to their strengths. All the key indicators of their career success -- their celebrity popularity index scores, the number of positive stories about their exploits and their corporate endorsement dollars -- all declined dramatically. And they were only able to regain their career momentum when they refocused their attention back to what they did best – leveraging their basketball gifts.

There is an important lesson here. In most careers, like sports, politics or business, you achieve success by concentrating on your strengths.

This is also true in HR. The two biggest mistakes that an HR professional can make are:

1. **Wasting time trying to improve their weaknesses.**
2. **Not spending enough time building on their strengths.**

The logic of building on your strengths comes from the terrific research done by Martin Seligman who along with his colleagues used it to make their mark in positive psychology. In their research, they reasoned that rather than trying to address your weaknesses, you'll have much more success and positive experiences when you identify your strengths and capitalize on them. I have also been inspired by the work of Chuck Maniscalco, my former CEO at Quaker Tropicana Gatorade, who attributes much of his own career success and progression to growing his own strengths into towering ones and advocating vigorously that all leaders do the same.

However, sadly, like Michael and Magic, many HR people don't follow this path. They move into jobs that don't play to their natural gifts. And as a result, they lose ground in advancing their careers because these roles don't allow them to showcase those abilities they can really do well.

To further illustrate this point, let me share...

How Mike Cohen Turned One Very Specialized Skill Into A Successful Senior Executive Role in HR

Mike is a friend, former boss and mentor of mine. He's also the best trainer, coach and group facilitator I've ever seen. He is an example of this "go small and grow big" idea. In Mike's case, early in his career, he went small and specialized in group facilitation. And he got so great at it that he was able to leverage it into a position as vice president of human resources development at Quaker Oats.

Here's his story.

After getting his masters in business and marketing from University of Illinois, Mike landed a position in marketing at his first firm, but then was reassigned to a special temporary project addressing union problems. This was his first exposure to HR work. And, in two more HR-related jobs over five years, he gained significant, diverse functional experience working with employees in manufacturing sites, nonunion environments, bank operations, sales and marketing. But what he gained from a career standpoint was even more valuable. He learned that the one part of all these jobs he really enjoyed most was the time he spent facilitating groups.

Over the ensuing months and years, Mike followed this passion and decided to build his facilitation skills. He looked for opportunities to facilitate and completed a number of facilitation certification programs. And shortly thereafter, attracted by the opportunity to do more facilitation, he joined Quaker Oats as a training manager.

While at Quaker, Mike began using and marketing his facilitation skills further. He created and taught a series of management development training classes that became mandatory for middle and senior managers. These classes weren't lecture-based, but instead were highly interactive, based on adult learning principles and enabled Mike to leverage his facilitation talents to engage these managers in the learning process.

As a result of the tremendous success and positive feedback from these training sessions, Mike's reputation spread inside the organization -- all the way to the C-suite. And before long, senior executives began contacting Mike directly and requesting that he facilitate business strategy meetings for their teams, new product innovation meetings, sales meetings for their managers and customers, culture initiatives, productivity improvement sessions and succession planning meetings. He quickly became the organization's go-to person for facilitating senior level meetings.

But Mike didn't stop there.

Rather than hoard his skills, he began to share them. He started doing train-the-trainers, one-on-one coaching and certification sessions for other HR professionals and managers interested in facilitating their own business meetings. And, rather than go solo, he often reached out to partner with his HR colleagues on many of these facilitation assignments.

Over time, these efforts paid off. He was promoted to vice president of human resources development and asked to head up talent development initiatives for all of Quaker's global businesses. In this role, Mike built an entire HR function consisting of professional trainers, OD specialists, and executive development consultants. And if that wasn't enough, for a period of time, he was also asked to step in and lead the corporate staffing and diversity groups.

Like Tiger Woods in golf, Mike was able to leverage one single skill into rock star status at Quaker Oats, building an entire empire within HR well beyond his one core specialty.

"Anytime you can become an expert in an area, you become the person that everyone goes to for information, and that immediately can make you invaluable," Mike told me recently.

"However, it's important that as you do this you don't alienate your HR colleagues. You want to collaborate and combine efforts whenever possible. Remember, as you're building your career everyone can be an ally. Anyone can be a resource to you. It's not a zero sum game. If you allow them to share in your success, more success will come to you as a result."

With that philosophy, it's easy to see why Mike enjoyed a successful twenty-five year career at Quaker Oats. Today, Mike is President, Michael L. Cohen Associates and leverages his facilitation skills in his own firm as a consultant, trainer, and executive coach on leadership, conflict management, organization diagnosis, change management, team development, board governance, and organization development. He has also expanded his influence as a member of the executive education faculty at several Chicago universities.

There Are A Number Of Lessons You Can Learn From The "Good" Tiger Woods and Mike Cohen Examples

Don't be afraid to go small by specializing and "nicheing" yourself. There are few things that can have a greater impact on your HR career than building your reputation as an expert in one area. It could be in a well-established specialty like labor relations, compensation or employee benefits plans. Or it could be in a narrower specialty or micro-niche within HR such as work life programs or recruiting talent using social networks. The key is to find a particular niche that both appeals to you and is valued by your organization. Then resolve to spend time developing your knowledge and abilities in this niche so that you can be viewed as the "leading authority."

When you go small, you become the "go to" person for that area. When you are known as the leader or the expert, people will automatically seek you out for advice and information. Soon you'll become a valuable part of the HR information network in your company or industry. As part of this network, you'll find that you're able to get information and support that you need much more quickly and you'll find out sooner about opportunities that can help you advance your career.

When going small, go where your passion calls out to you. Whatever you decide to focus on should be more than a job for you. If you've going to invest all your time, talent and energy in an endeavor, your heart should be in it too. It should become a mission or passion for you. Passion isn't confined to the bedroom. When you have passion in your heart about your specialty, it lifts your entire life. Days go by faster and your work becomes more interesting and enjoyable. You have more stamina, more resilience, and more commitment in everything you do. Passion can take you from merely being competent to being outstanding. Fueling the passion and fire in your heart is an important step towards taking your HR career to the next level.

Going small is not enough if your area of focus does not create value for those you lead or your organization. Mike Cohen's skills in facilitation would have been worthless if Quaker executives didn't view them as a way to help reach their goals. As an HR professional, you can focus on your strengths in recruiting, team building, employee advocacy or any other noble attribute. But unless you can apply your strengths in ways that create value for others, you've wasted your time.

Don't know what you should go small in? Ask someone. Many of us have a "blind spot" when it comes to our own strengths, passions or specialties. You may have been struggling with self-examination for years, but a peer, boss or mentor who gets to know you over the period of a week could probably point out your strong points fairly easily. The hard part is hearing, and then accepting what you hear. Once you do know what you were intended to do, make a plan to put that to work.

Go small the old-fashion way – earn it. Be prepared to work hard soaking up, digesting and reapplying every drop of information about the area you've chosen to specialize in. So read, watch, write about, and listen to everything you can get your hands on concerning your specialty area. Attend lectures, conventions, and training even if you have to pay your own way. Join industry-related organizations and clubs. Blog. Give presentations and speeches. Author articles. Develop power point presentations. Most HR people don't consciously strive to become experts. They attain that level of expertise because their level of interest in their specialty transcends their job.

Do a passion check annually. I encourage HR people everywhere to pop their heads up once a year to analyze if they're excited about the work they're doing and the organization that's paying them to do it. This applies to your area of specialty as well. It's career advice many of us give our clients that we should follow ourselves. You can't get too busy to do this. It's easy to get bogged down in the daily grind and not take a day out to assess whether your focus area is taking you where you want to go. You need to be energized by the constant opportunity in front of you to do new things, learn new things, and be involved with different people. Otherwise, you can lose your passion for your niche and your commitment to be super-successful within it.

Avoid organizations and managers who only want to fix what's wrong. When developing talent, some organizations focus exclusively on fixing what's wrong and let strengths take care of themselves. In these companies, business leaders spend most of their time working with their weakest performing people trying to improve them, while ignoring their strengths. Even in organizations like GE or Pepsi, known for developing world-class HR talent, there are managers within them that are glass-half empty maniacs mentally wired to pounce on people's shortcomings. So, one word of advice: avoid them. How often have you heard, "She's a great leader, an excellent presenter and terrific at building teams. But we need to put a plan together to address her time management and follow up skills." Let's analyze this: Where's the emphasis? However, where is the greatest area for potential growth? They are not the same! In general, trying to work on your weakest attributes only leads to negative self-esteem and frustration, especially if your mammoth strengths are being neglected.

Let someone else work on your deficiencies. This brings up the point of improving your weaknesses. Don't spend a lot of time doing this. Let someone else do that for you. It can be very alluring to think of yourself as an HR professional capable of handling anything with flair and having no shortcomings. That's a pipe dream. Nobody can do everything well. Most of us are lucky if we can do ONE thing passably well. So if your biggest weakness is that you don't manage time well or don't follow up as much as you should, don't fall into the trap of becoming a better clerical employee. Hire one, befriend one, delegate or pass these tasks work on to a colleague that can do this better than you can.

If you are hell-bent on being a jack of all trades, then become a master of ONE. There are some HR professionals that hesitate to go small. They like the variety that comes with being a 100% pure HR generalist and believe that going small limits their options within HR. I'm a firm believer in following your passion. So, rather than argue with this "jack of all trades" perspective, I would suggest that you meet me half way. Resolve to become a generalist…but with a major in at least one area of specialty. In doing this, you'll find that your expertise and confidence in this one area will help sustain you in situations where your specialized knowledge is more urgently needed than your more general HR perspectives. You'll also find that you can fall back on your experiences in this specialty when you need to demonstrate your competence quickly in unfamiliar situations. For example, if you're in the middle of big meeting about cutting costs in manufacturing, being able to weigh in with a perspective on the effectiveness of the incentive pay plans (if your specialty is comp) or the company's flexibility in subcontracting out union work (if labor relations is your specialty) can establish you as a player early in these discussions.

Share your knowledge. One of Mike Cohen's success strategies was sharing his expertise with colleagues, clients, superiors, everyone. This is a practice you should emulate. Make sure, that when you share your knowledge, you do it to benefit others. As Mike did, there's no reason why you can't run train-the-trainers or coach others on your specialty. Write a blog and articles on things you're good at; attend industry events in your specialty; make connections with movers and shakers in your niche; learn the HR trends and buzzwords that will position you as an "expert" in your area of expertise. Even in social settings talk about your specialty, when people ask what you do. By taking these types of actions, when you DO decide to make your move, you'll be known, have a robust network, and great support system that will enable you to quickly move into new career opportunities that leverage your strengths.

<u>Unwritten HR Rule #5</u>
Go small to grow big.

Don't be afraid to specialize and niche yourself in HR. Go where your passion calls out to you, but make sure your HR specialty is valued by your organization or by other companies. If you absolutely must become a jack of all trades, then also become a master of ONE.

"One secret to being the best in the world is to make the 'world' smaller."

6

HOW TO ACE YOUR NEXT PERFORMANCE REVIEW

To become a serious contender for the biggest and baddest HR roles, you need to establish a consistent track record of acing year-end performance reviews. However, this can be extremely challenging because...

Most Performance Reviews Take Into Account Factors You Don't Totally Control!

In many companies, the financial success of the business and how your peers perform will determine *your* final appraisal rating. These are two elements you obviously can't fully influence. For example, in some organizations even if you perform well, but the business does badly, your performance rating (along with everyone else's) may be lowered. In other cases, you are force-ranked against your peers in order to allocate limited merit dollars and your "above requirements" rating can be lowered to "meets requirements" because you came out on the bad end of the peer-to-peer comparisons. This can be frustrating.

A senior HR colleague of mine experienced this exasperation personally after her year-end review. She had been rated a "3" on her company's 5-point scale, which was "average." With that in mind, she signed off on the review and was told at that time that her performance was "solid" and that everything was fine.

However, what happened next was brutal.

She was called back in a few weeks later and given the pink slip! While she knew her performance wasn't stellar, she clearly didn't see this coming and was shocked beyond belief. She was told that, after reviewing her performance more closely and weighing that against the company's financial troubles and her peers, the higher ups decided to whack her job.

While I'm not going to call out her company here - that ain't my style - suffice it to say that if you're an HR professional, you can't take performance reviews for granted. And, you can't afford to be lazy in preparing for them.

All organizations go through cycles where they feel the financial pinch to cut headcount. And, many companies use annual reviews more than ever to weed out low performing HR folks as well as those they'll elevate in the organization.

So, if you want to get the best possible review, you need to prepare well in advance...starting now! To that end, here are nine actions that can help you jump start the process of nailing your next performance review:

#1: Start tracking and documenting, immediately! Don't wait until the end of the year to gather your results. Start today by creating a folder on your desktop and use it to save all the e-mail feedback and kudos you receive from customers, peers, and managers throughout the year — including your boss, his or her boss, and all other leaders between you and the CEO. This will ensure that you've got all your accomplishments captured in one spot. It's easy for an overworked boss to forget how excited she was about that great new mentoring program you launched in February – if your review is not until November.

#2: Get signoff on your upcoming year's performance objectives and key deliverables, now! Don't wait on your boss to get the process started. If you don't have an agreed-on set of performance goals established for the upcoming year, take the initiative to put them on paper and get your manager's approval, pronto. If you support internal clients, include their expectations as well. Like most managers, he or she will take your internal clients' views to heart at review time, so you'll want to make sure that everyone is on the same page.

#3: Make sure you're working on the right stuff by checking in regularly. Don't take for granted that your amazing accomplishments are warming your boss' heart — even if you're following a game plan they've laid out! In tough times, HR priorities shift quickly. And, it's wise to check in at least once a month to make sure your major, burning-hot priorities are the same as your manager's.

The top performance ratings go to those people who are working on mission-critical assignments. So, providing regular updates to your boss will help ensure that you're one of the folks plugged into these do-or-die missions.

And, one other thing that is important to note. Although most bosses wait until the end of the year to actually write or submit your review, they may be required to submit your performance rating and your merit raise recommendation well before then. So, this is another good reason to actively and objectively communicate your performance highlights throughout the year.

#4: If you got a bad review last time, get help – now! If your last review was not what you wanted, it's time to put this situation behind you. Yes, it may have been unfair. Yes, your boss might have been a prick. Or one of your clients may have had an ax to grind. But, get over it. It's time to look forward and get some guidance.

Visit with your boss, your clients, your colleagues well before review time and ask, "What can I do to improve my performance?" If your colleagues demur, tell them "I'm serious; this is not the time to be nice to me. I'm asking for help. What could I be doing to become better at my job?" You don't have to treat this as personal confession time and tell them that your prior year's review was crummy – that's none of their business — just focus on getting their suggestions for improvement.

#5: To get a top rating you must be prepared to show clear business impact. It is not enough to say that you've done a bunch of stuff. You have to connect these activities to important business objectives. Only then do they become results that have impact at review time. So, you will want to arm yourself with hard data.

You want to say things like, "before I started, we had X problems and since my Y work we've improved that number Z%". Then really seal the deal by saying that, in your opinion, your contributions have helped achieve some larger organizational goal like reducing costs or improving retention. Make sure your boss knows that you understand how your work is contributing to addressing the organization's key issues.

#6: Do your own "self-appraisals" each month. Conduct your own monthly mini-reviews before you meet with your manager. Be honest with yourself — evaluate how well you are progressing against your objectives. Summarize what you've accomplished and give yourself a rating each month. If you do these monthly "mini-appraisals," you shouldn't be surprised at the end of the year.

Be objective and evaluate the dents and dings in your performance too. That is, dust-ups you've had with coworkers, missed deadlines and situations where you were just off your game. You want to avoid surprise hits and anticipate answers in advance if you need to explain your shortfalls. The beauty of monthly self-appraisals are that they give you time to make mid-course corrections early during the year, if you feel yourself getting off track.

#7: Focus on quantifying your contributions. When the time comes to write up or give input on your final review, many HR folks simply list everything they did during the year. They believe that volume is all that's needed to get that top rating. So they submit pages upon pages of completed activities. It reads like a detailed job description. And, guess what? That's exactly what it is. Most of that stuff is what you're already paid to do. And is a waste of time.

As you know, the top rating is a reward for exceptional performance, not doing your job. So when you list your achievements take time and focus on the net impact on the business. Did you negotiate the new union labor contract below your company's approved budgeted costs? Did you reduce the cost of turnover in the customer service department as a result of the new job rotation program you put in place for customer care specialists? Did you architect a new, out-of-the box approach to college recruiting which dramatically improved cost-per-hire and quality-of-hire? Whatever you did, make a case for your beyond-the-call-of-duty contributions.

Sorry, doing the job you're paid to do for yet another year is just table stakes – and will only get you an average (or below average) rating in tough times. It is certainly not justification for the top review.

#8: Distinguish yourself from your peers and use BIPPs. As mentioned previously, just doing your job well isn't a compelling enough reason to hand you the top rating. So don't expect it! Remember, most managers have a specific budget to use for ratings and raises so a high rating or increase for you means a smaller one for your peers. If your organization is like Pepsi, you will be ranked against your peers when your company calibrates what ratings to give.

So, when you are gathering your accomplishments, make sure they focus on ways you may have differentiated yourself from your coworkers, where you took on additional unplanned responsibilities, or where you stepped up without being asked and completed a particularly challenging project that was beyond the scope of your job.

In most cases, to *really* emerge from the pack, you will need to execute -- and preferably lead -- at least one BIPP during the year. A BIPP is a "bold, innovative power project." BIPPs are ground-breaking, out-of-the-box, breakthrough HR initiatives that are clearly visible and set your organization on fire. If you've not identified your annual BIPP, you need to do it now.

To generate BIPP ideas, talk to your boss and your clients. Or Google "best HR ideas" or "best HR innovations" and check out the top award-winning HR ideas launched last year from other organizations. *HR Executive* magazine runs a feature on these ideas every year. From these various sources, there should be a few ideas you can steal and potentially re-apply within your own organization as your BIPP.

#9: Learn to deal with the pressure and strain of continually going above and beyond what's expected. Chasing results daily, every quarter, every year is stressful. Sometimes it seems nothing is ever good enough. Goals are set higher each year and the performance bar is always rising. At Pepsi, the pace was like greased lightning, with many bright, hard-driving HR personalities going full speed all the time. The pressure to learn new approaches to generate results was and is high.

But it's important to recognize that nobody can be in "sprint mode" all the time. It's crucial that you take time to "pull up" once in a while to celebrate accomplishments with the individuals you work with and take personal time off to "recharge your batteries." This is a major factor in sustaining your high performance over the long haul.

To conclude, in tough times, falling in the average performer category puts your HR job and career at risk. Hopefully, following these steps starting now can help you max out your performance rating when review time comes...and put you in the running for the more significant HR roles in the future.

Unwritten HR Rule #6

To give yourself an edge as a serious contender for the biggest and baddest HR roles, you need to establish a consistent track record of acing your performance reviews. And to do this, you must: document and do self-appraisals consistently, check in with your boss regularly, show clear business impact, quantify your contributions, and make sure you have at least one BIPP that clearly differentiates you from the rest of your peers.

7

WHAT TO DO WHEN YOU
MESS UP IN HR

Here are a few important lessons I've learned from watching entirely too many movies:

- Never assume a deranged killer is dead just because he's been shot 26 times in the chest.
- Do not panic if your plane has been hijacked by terrorists – a regular passenger will easily be able to land the plane with help from the control tower.
- Before solving a case, the police officer always winds up angrily slamming down his badge on the captain's desk.
- No matter how powerful the bad guy is – if he's truly evil, he'll never win.

While this may be a little naïve, I don't think bad guys win in HR either. So as tempting as it might be to secure your next promotion by concealing your screw-ups and behaving underhandedly, in the long run it takes a lot more than that to be successful.

If there's one thing you can learn from the movies, it's that big mistakes and treachery are almost always uncovered. So take your inspiration from the big screen and avoid being sleazy.

Unfortunately, Stephanie Jensen didn't learn this lesson soon enough. Awhile back, Stephanie was a rising star with a great track record in Human Resources. She became Brocade Communications Systems' vice president for human resources after 20 years in HR jobs at high-tech companies.

She had come a long way and had a lot to be proud of after starting off in an entry-level position at Apple Computer.

Unfortunately, her HR career took a detour that she hadn't planned when....

Stephanie Jensen, This Former VP HR, Was Sentenced To Four Months In Federal Prison And Fined $1,250,000.00!

You might wonder...what the heck happened?

Unfortunately, she was found guilty of conspiring to backdate employees' stock options. And, along with the President of the company, she was convicted of lying about the impact these actions had on the company's finances. So not only were her actions as an HR leader found to be illegal, she was also caught lying.

I wish I could say that this is an isolated case, but sadly it isn't. According to *HR Executive*...

Here Are Eight More HR Leaders You've Probably Never Heard Of, Who Were Charged Or Convicted of Criminal Behavior

William Sinclair Jr., an HR executive with the Library of Congress, was charged in December 2008 with conspiracy, wire fraud and identity theft for allegedly stealing names from the agency's database and passing them on to his cousin.

Gregory Horton, former executive VP of HR for America Online, pled guilty in 2005 and did time for scamming AOL and others by billing for millions of dollars in phantom services.

Nancy Tullos, former HR vice president for Broadcom Corporation, pled guilty to the role she played in an illegal stock-option backdating scandal involving Henry Nicholas, co-founder of the company, who was convicted in 2008.

Gary A. Ray, former vice president and head of HR at KB Home, pled guilty in February 2009 to falsifying reports and conspiring with CEO and Chairman Bruce E. Karatz to obstruct a Securities and Exchange Commission investigation into yet another case of stock-option backdating.

Dennis M. Dowd, former senior manager of corporate benefits for Hitachi America, pled guilty in March to setting up a fake bank account and stealing $6.1 million from the healthcare plan between 2000 and 2008.

Elizabeth Billmeyer, human resources manager at Agriprocessors, a kosher meat-packing plant, pled guilty after being charged in March to harboring undocumented alien workers for profit.

Alejandro Urrutia-Garcia, HR manager for Universal Industrial Sales Inc., got 36 months of probation in February for helping undocumented workers get jobs.

Christian Deeb Rahaim, a former human resources executive at Enron, was sentenced to five years and three months for wire fraud in 2007 after scamming nearly $3 million from the company. His crimes were committed years after Enron went bankrupt following what is now considered the mother of all ethical meltdowns -- the accounting scandal at the then-energy giant that was revealed in October 2001.

Granted, chances are (hopefully) you'll never rise to this level of stupid criminal behavior. And, clearly when the company you are a part of partakes in obvious illegal activity, it's time to not only to say no, but time to find a new company.

But, that's not the point.

The point is this...

Every day in your HR life there are itty-bitty opportunities to: shade the truth, hide the facts, misrepresent how much progress you're making on a project to your boss, or breach your client's confidentially by gossiping...to name just a few. One of my early HR managers told me to not worry about this: "These are just the little white lies that come with the HR territory."

With all due respect to her: Nothing could be further from the truth.

Nothing can derail a promising HR career quicker than falling into these little traps. I've seen far too many great HR folks get exposed, disgraced and shown the door because they lied or played loosy goosy with the facts.

It goes without saying that as an HR professional you have an inherent ethical responsibility to your leaders, employees and stockholders (or owners) to always do what's right....even if it costs you your position.

A division president I reported to once told me...

"As Our HR Leader, I Expect You To Be The Conscience Of The Organization. Your Ethical Standards Need To Be Higher Than Anyone Else On My Management Team. I Know That Doesn't Seem Fair, But If You Can't Accept That, Then Let's Talk About Finding You Another Job."

That is what makes the true HR professional so critical and so valuable...the ability to be the trusted compass of the organization.

But let's face it: stuff happens in Human Resources. Nobody's perfect. We're all human. I've screwed up more times than I can count. We all mess up.

But lean in and listen closely. Here's the unwritten HR rule in all this...

If You Mess Up, Fess Up. Fast!

And tell the whole truth. Tell the truth to anyone you can fess up to: your boss, your people, your clients, the receptionist, the guy at the bar, your cat. Everyone. THEN, GET ON WITH YOUR LIFE, with a clear conscience.

Yes, fess up.

Do it on little things.

Do it on big things.

It doesn't matter.

If you haven't finished that turnover report your boss asked for – fess up, fast.

If you made a mistake calculating the salary increase for an important senior executive – fess up, fast.

If you've already told 2,000 employees...by mistake...about a great new backup day care program they're now *not* going to get – don't try to take back or lie about what you said, just fess up, fast.

(And to answer the question you no doubt are asking: Yes, I've fessed up to all of these things).

And you should too. No excuses. No "re-positioning" of the facts. No CYA.

But, let's be clear: "telling the truth" is not an easy and painless thing to do. It's uncomfortable and from personal experience, I'll admit that you may walk around for days feeling stupid. However, it's a whole lot better than walking around in a 12×12 jail cell or in a nice looking outplacement office.

Often in HR we have to deliver bad news. It's fine to put a positive spin on a very unpleasant situation, but you must always be clear, honest and upfront, even in the toughest circumstance. There's a line between conveying things in a positive way and lying. And, you don't want to cross that line.

Telling the truth ASAP may be the most career enhancing thing you can do after a screw up.

People have massive amounts of forgiveness in their hearts for sins — including stupid sins. But they hate like hell folks who won't come clean with the truth. You need to look no further than Bernard Madoff, Marion Jones, Barry Bonds, Pete Rose, O.J. Simpson, Bill Clinton, Kelvin Sampson, and Roger Clemens to see how not telling the truth killed their reputations overnight!

If you don't want to be the HR person that joins that group... or the group of infamous HR leaders mentioned earlier...when you mess up, fess up, fast.

It's one of the best career decisions you'll ever make.

<u>Unwritten HR Rule #7</u>

When you mess up, fess up. Fast!

"In HR as in life...when you have a problem, if you tell the truth the problem becomes part of your past. If you lie it becomes part of your future."

8

A SIMPLE 5-MINUTE CAREER INVESTMENT YOU SHOULD MAKE EACH WEEK

Recently, I was talking over lunch with an HR colleague of mine who heads up college recruiting at another company.

She shared with me an amazing story that has huge implications for advancing your career in HR.

Apparently, she was looking to hire a Human Resources master's degree candidate for a lucrative, full-time, fast-track position in her organization.

The job had just about everything you'd want. Great pay. Great benefits. Great company. Great location. Awesome future. A job most HR folks I know would have killed to get right out of grad school.

Anyway, she then went online to check out this promising candidate. At Facebook, she found the candidate's Fan page with this description of his interests: "smokin' blunts" (cigars hollowed out and stuffed with marijuana), shooting people and obsessive sex, all described in vivid slang.

And, her jaw dropped!

It didn't matter that this candidate was clearly showboating.

It didn't matter that this is somehow a badge of honor among some college students who have this weird competition on who can come across as the craziest online.

It all didn't matter.

As far as my colleague, the head of recruiting was concerned...he was done. Finished. History. No job offer.

This All Happened Because This HR Job Candidate Did Not Take His Online Image And Reputation Seriously!

Even though I wasn't involved in this situation, my question to this guy would simply be: What the heck were you thinking about?

It is absolutely no secret that most companies are checking out profiles on LinkedIn and googling candidates to conduct quick and dirty background checks. They do it for college students. They do it for HR managers. They do it HR directors, HR VPs and senior HR VPs. Most times they find nothing to disqualify a candidate.

However, many organizations are digging deeper...especially candidates for entry-level positions. They are looking up applicants on sites like Facebook, Twitter, YouTube, Google+ and other social networking hangouts where some unaware job candidates post risqué or provocative comments or photographs about drinking, recreational drug use and sexual exploits in what they mistakenly believe is relative privacy. What can show up there can make an otherwise great candidate look immature, unprofessional and a high risk hire.

What does this mean for you? Why am I telling you this? Here's why...

It doesn't matter if you're a college student or not, if you're interviewing for any Human Resources job -- from HR Manager to HR SVP and everything else in between -- don't think for a second that the person you're interviewing with for one hour isn't going to take another five seconds to at least Google you.

You might say – great, Google me. You're not going to find anything. And you know what...

If You Are Googled And Nothing
Shows Up, That's EVEN WORSE!

It means that you probably don't have a web site ...that you probably have never given a speech to a prominent organization ...that you probably have not written any HR articles ...that you probably have never done any work of note in the community or with a charity ...that you probably have never held a prominent role in a HR professional organization ...that you have not done anything that has distinguished you professionally within your company ...or anywhere else for that matter.

That's what it *could* mean when nothing shows up.

Now understand, none of this may be true. But that's how you could be perceived. And that may not be fair. But that's reality.

On the other hand, I've just given you an important, career-changing tip for success. If you have disgusting and unflattering stuff about you popping up online, take steps right now to get rid of it.

If nothing shows up when your name is googled, then do this: Create your own web site, speak at an HR workshop, write articles and have them published online, involve yourself in the community, get involved in professional associations, take on the leadership role in noteworthy activities in your organization. Since you are going to get googled anyway...and possibly LinkedIn, MySpaced, Facebooked or Twittered...you want to take charge of managing your image online.

These strategies will all work in the long-term to brand you positively online.

But, what about right now?

Here are some additional strategies for enhancing your online reputation immediately...

#1: Make sure your LinkedIn profile page stays up to date. If you're not on LinkedIn (hint, hint!), you're a dinosaur, so sign up now. If you are on LinkedIn, providing current information on your profile page (see Chapter 9) increases your visibility online and helps you build your professional brand. That means that anyone looking for information about you on the web, will find everything they need to know at a glance - your skills, your employment information, your contact details, and so on. That's why it's important to make sure that your LinkedIn profile is complete, detailed, and truly represents you. However, if you really want to optimize your LinkedIn online profile, take these actions...

- **Fill in your personal details**. Create a detailed profile including all your personal details, such as country, industry, etc. Don't forget to enter your current job position (company and title), because that's right at the top of the page when someone views your profile.
- **Write about yourself**. Use your online profile to help people find all the relevant information about you. Include all the keywords and skills from your resume in your "About" section. That will make it easier for your profile to be found in online search results.
- **Add a photo**. You can add a photo (a headshot is recommended) to your online profile to add credibility to your profile.
- **Add links**. The links section of your profile is a good way to provide even more information to people who view your profile. Add links to your company web site, your blog, and to your favorite sites.
- **Add your contact details**. Provide additional information on how to reach you, such as your e-mail address, phone number, and office number in the business details section to make it easy for you to get connected with others.

#2: If you are member of an HR association or club, encourage the leaders to list all member names (including yours) on their official website. A friend of mine, who is an HR director in Chicago for a non-profit association, is also on the leadership committee of the NAAAHR (National Association of African American HR Professionals). Her name appears prominently when you search online for the roster of that site.

Many associations list bios and pictures of their members on their website. You might also want to encourage your employer to do the same. Most large companies won't do this unless you're a member of senior management. However, some small companies will include information on their website for all professional-level employees. It's worth a shot.

#3: Increase your online exposure by writing short articles and submitting them to free article directories. The more times your name appears in online search results, the better. You want your name to pop up in multiple places when someone googles you. This gives you legitimacy and tells people that you are a busy, important HR professional.

A great way to accomplish this and boost your credibility online is to write short articles (300-500 words) about some HR topic and submit them to free article directories. The most popular article directory is ezinearticles.com.

For example, if you are an HR generalist, you could write an article about *"7 Ways To Succeed With Your Clients as An HR Generalist,"* or *"10 Top Competencies Needed By Any HR Generalist."*

If you are a compensation specialist, you might write an article about *"How To Get Peer Companies To Participate in Community Wage Surveys,"* or *"How To Keep Compensation Costs Flat In A Recessionary Economy."*

These articles could be about anything in your area of specialty in HR.

The key is that you'll want to include a short bio about yourself as the author at the end of the article. Google loves content and anything posted in ezinearticles.com gets picked up and posted online quickly. Putting 5 to 10 articles on this site is a great strategy because your name and your article, once they've been approved (which usually takes a few days), will get posted on Google within 1-2 days. A side benefit is that other ezine publishers can also pick up your article and re-print it, thereby spreading your name virally across the web. But the most important benefit is that your articles enable you to put your best foot forward. And provide a variety of places you can be found online when recruiters, executives and hiring managers background check your reputation.

To get started, simply go to ezinearticles.com, review their Author Terms of Service, the Editorial Guides and then create a free Basic membership account so that you can send in your first article today. Again, all of this is free. The whole process should only take a few minutes, but the promotion and career exposure you'll receive is priceless.

#4: If you're on sites like Facebook or Twitter, police your online image and scrub it clean. Being judged by the images on your Facebook page or the tweets appearing on your Twitter account may seem inappropriate and unethical. After all, your online social network is part of your private life and has nothing to do with your HR job. Right? Wrong. You and I live in an age where we are both one Google search away from having anything posted online about our private life exposed to anyone with a PC. For some companies, that's enough for them to conclude that the lines between your personal life and professional life blur. They will argue that as an HR professional on their payroll, you are a living, breathing ambassador of their company. And, if you look bad online, they look bad.

Whether this is right or wrong is irrelevant. The only way to protect yourself is to control your online image and be careful whom you call or accept as a "friend." Don't allow people you barely know to post stuff on your site. Tell every one of your "friends" that you'll remove them from your list if they post lewd photos or obscene images, photos of people getting drunk, skinny dipping or the like. People may think you're paranoid, but a little piece of information that the HR higher ups see or hear about may be the tipping point causing them to wonder whether you're serious about your career or a slacker.

So, you should take a few minutes every month to Google yourself online. You might be surprised at what you find out. Also, take a few minutes each week to examine ways to make your background and experience look better online. Writing a couple of articles a year and posting them on ezinearticles.com is a great investment that can enhance your reputation when people are going online to check you out.

An executive career coach that I talk to frequently sums up the key message in this chapter quite well when she says...

"In Today's World, You Are Who Google Says You Are!"

Which begs this question..."who is Google saying YOU are?" Find out. Google yourself - now! While you're at it, check out all the social networking sites you're on. Right away.

Extra Bonus Tip! Google has a service that automatically notifies you when something is posted online with any key words that you request (like your name). It's called Google alert. By entering your name, anything *new* and floating around the internet about you allows you to be the first to know. *Homework for today:* go to http://www.google.com/alerts and setup an alert for your name!

<u>Unwritten HR Rule #8</u>

It's important that you look good online. Take five minutes per week to Google your name to check and protect your online HR image. Carefully watch your Facebook and Twitter postings. Use ezinearticles.com to broaden your online exposure and reputation. Set up a Google alert for your name.

9

15 SNEAKY LITTLE WAYS TO TAKE YOUR HR CAREER TO THE NEXT LEVEL USING THE WORLD'S MOST POWERFUL CAREER MANAGEMENT TOOL

With over 60 million members, LinkedIn.com has become the most powerful tool on the planet for managing your career.

It's also huge for HR with over 700,000 human resources professionals who currently belong to the LinkedIn network.

However, based on talks I've had recently with many of my HR colleagues, very few of them are maximizing the value of LinkedIn. A lot of them barely use it once they sign up. And, even more HR folks are not even signed up at all! Let me tell you, if you're in this group, and want to enhance your career in HR, you're missing the boat. Big time.

Since I've been a part of the LinkedIn universe, I've picked up some amazing insights into the ways a handful of human resources managers have been very quietly using this tool to advance their HR careers.

And, I thought, hey, why not share these with you and other HR folks so that everyone can benefit. There are at least 2 or 3 of these tips you can get value from - whether you're an entry level HR generalist or a C-suite HR senior executive.

So, without further ado, here's my list of 15 sneaky, amazing but brilliant little ways your HR colleagues are using LinkedIn to advance their careers — and how you can too. Enjoy.

#1: Use LinkedIn to help you ace your next HR job interview. People who will interview you for an HR job will know a lot about you from your resume (and by googling you) long before you set ever foot on their hallowed ground. Why not use LinkedIn to turn the tables and check out all the people on your interview schedule too? Knowing who went to your same school, who likes to golf, who is reading the latest Ulrich book, or who knows the same people you know is a heck of a lot better than an awkward silence after, "I'm doing fine, thank you."

#2: Get the inside scoop on the job you're interviewing for. Some HR folks are discreetly checking out the people who used to have the job that they're interviewing for. You can do this too by going to the "People" tab and searching for job title and company, and by checking the "Past titles" box only. Now, this doesn't work all this time, and it doesn't work at all if this job isn't listed in their profile. However, if you do strike gold doing this, you can use this information to reach out and contact the people who used to hold this position, and get the inside scoop on the job, the manager and what growth potential exists for that role. Frankly, I'm not gutsy enough to do all this, but many aggressive HR job-seekers I know have.

#3: Get the inside dope on the company you're interviewing with. Perform an advanced search for company name and check the "Past" box. This will enable you to get a rough idea of what turnover looks like and whether or not folks seem to be bailing out of this organization like rats from a sinking ship.

#4: Get up to speed fast in your new HR job. One of the toughest challenges any HR person faces is getting up to speed quickly in a new job. It doesn't matter what kind of job it is. When you start a new job, ordinarily your roots aren't that deep in that new role. And if you're joining a new company, it's even tougher. You face the hurdles of learning the new culture, building new relationships and trying to establish chemistry with people when you're the stranger from outside. With LinkedIn, if you're the new HR kid on the block, you can study your new colleagues' profiles and quickly use that info to find areas of common ground, ways you might be able to support them in their careers and ways to establish rapport with them more quickly.

#5: Determine how competitive you are for the next HR promotion. When a new promotional opportunity opens up, it would be great to know how your background, training, experience and the size of your network compares with that of others who may be competing with you for this position too. Now you can. In addition, some HR professionals have found it especially helpful to see how their peers explain what they do in HR and what they choose to highlight about their HR experience and non-work lives. One person confided to me that she's probably updated her profile 7-8 times based on something she's seen on her peer's profile.

#6: Scope out the resume of someone who beat you out for a job. If you've been passed over, you can walk around angry at the world. Or you can learn from it. If you've ever wondered what the resume looks like of someone who got the job you wanted -- well, now you can find out.

#7: Position yourself as a subject matter expert in your area of HR expertise. If you want to make your mark in specialized areas like compensation, labor relations, OD, staffing or benefits, LinkedIn makes this a lot easier. Here are the steps you can take to do this:

(a) Get recommended as an expert resource by asking those who value your insights to write a testimonial that promotes you (and them!).

(b) Start regularly posting questions in the Answers area.

(c) Regularly answer relevant questions with specific information based on your expertise and work your way up to becoming an expert by giving top-rated answers.

You'll find that by using the Questions and Answers feature of LinkedIn, you can start conversations, create community, and position yourself as a subject matter expert in a relatively short time.

#8: Keep your resume up to date – easily. Today, everyone in HR needs an up to date resume, on their hard drive, ready to send out at a moment's notice. Years ago, when I wrote my first resume, I did what everyone else did. I typed it out, went to Kinko's and had them make 200 copies on their nice, expensive, high-grade, shiny, off-white paper. Shiny so it would look slick and stand out. Then when I found a mistake, I had to type it up, edit it, print it out again, go back to Kinko's and repeat the process. After all that, I might have given out 12 copies - half of them to my family. Now, if I meet someone, I don't say "here's my shiny new resume." Instead, I say "here's my contact info" and provide them a link to my LinkedIn profile or if they're not on LinkedIn, I can use LinkedIn to auto-email them a copy of my profile. Easy.

#9: Differentiate your HR resume and experience from everyone else's. An HR headhunter told me recently that she is increasingly seeing HR resumes that contain testimonials about the candidate at the end of the document. In a competitive job market, HR job seekers are now using such comments from their references to elevate themselves from the rest of the pack. For example, imagine if you had 3 or 4 different testimonials at the end of your resume that read like this:

"Rarely in my career have I worked with a more positive, insightful, and supportive HR leader than Jill Doe. She has a deep

insight into the business, a passion for getting results and an approach to working with people that brings out their best. I would be thrilled if the opportunity presented itself to work with her again." — John Smith (Vice President - Human Resources at ABC, a division of XYZ) who worked with Jill at XYZ Corporation.

Since Linked-in testimonials are impossible to manipulate, all a user can do with an average testimonial is not add it to their profile — they cannot change it. That lends an air of authenticity to Linked-in testimonials, which is great. If you are a Linked-in user, get some testimonials and add them to your resume. Ideally, you should have testimonials for each job you have held. Linked-in testimonials will legitimize your claims of functional expertise, and they will help a hiring manager understand exactly where, how and when you've created value in the past.

#10: Help in your job search. If you've lost your job or you're seeking out a new opportunity, besides everything else I've talked about so far, you can use LinkedIn to...

- *Attract recruiters looking for people in your HR specialty.* Think about what search terms or keywords recruiters or hiring managers enter in the LinkedIn search box to look for people like you. Example: "Compensation Specialist," "Human Resources Generalist," "Recruiting Manager" or "Director - Organization Development," Make sure those terms are in your profile.
- *Find open HR jobs you're interested in.* Search for jobs on LinkedIn by looking at the second tab of results called "The Web." There are over 5 million total jobs listed -- tons of these opportunities are for HR folks.
- *More quickly gain entry into organizations you want to work for.* Type in the names of the 10 organizations you would like most to work for and see which of your contacts know people there or know people who know people there. Then contact them and ask for referrals.
- *Relocate to your dream location.* Search for people in the region you would like to live in. Under "Interested In" select

hiring managers. Contact people in your second degree. Instead of asking for a job, offer them something of value and ask to meet.

- *Get referrals from old classmates.* See what your former classmates are up to. Some may be in a position to hire you and may give preference to someone from the same alma mater.

#11: Fill up free time on your next business trip by connecting with people in your network. This is one of my personal favorites. Here's the situation: You have a business trip planned and you have some blocks of free time while you're there. You want to make good use of it by meeting some new people, preferably folks that might be relevant to your business or your career; or you want to meet up with some people that you've perhaps only met online. Maybe a former colleague or classmate lives there and you didn't even realize it. Having all your contacts all in one place via LinkedIn makes it easy just to e-mail them beforehand, and set it all up.

#12: Get the help and support you need to do your job better. The "what are you working on" feature can be a powerful way of getting help, support and guidance on work-related projects. If you're struggling trying to determine "how to best retain engineers during tough times" or looking for "best practices in rolling out elder care benefits," make it known to your network. There might be contacts in or outside of your network, which could offer assistance or make recommendations on service providers.

#13: Get noticed and recognized for the work you've done and can do. I've seen a lot of HR profiles that are sparse. Don't be lazy. You want a meaty profile that puts out on a silver platter what you've done and what you're capable of doing. If you want an example, go to my profile. Now, you don't have to write a novel or go overboard like I did. And, you may not want to go back to beginning of time in your job history like I did either.

But the point is to put enough information out there about your background, job history, and areas of interest so that people know what to contact you about. Write a summary section that clearly outlines your personal brand or HR specialty that gets people jazzed up about what you do. Many profiles on LinkedIn are just a shell with a name and a short chronology. You would never submit a resume to a potential employer that only listed employment and dates, so why in the heck would you use this tactic online when your information is available for millions of people to see? Take the time to create a robust profile. It will get you noticed.

#14: Build a network without making networking your full-time day job. Those who have used LinkedIn successfully will tell you that you need at least 50 connections. They'll also tell you that this doesn't mean you should connect to every single Tom, Dick or HR person who sends you an invitation. LinkedIn is most effective when you connect with:
- Your top HR contacts
- Important HR or business folks in your industry
- Co-workers
- Individuals you've worked with in the past
- People who know you well
- Headhunters or executive search consultants

These are the people who can help you find new career opportunities and pass on ideas that can improve your impact and success in your current role. LinkedIn doesn't replace traditional networking, it just facilitates it. Always supplement your online efforts with face-to-face networking.

#15: Instantly stay in touch with your network – whether it's 5 or 5000 people. I've saved the best for last. This is my favorite way to use LinkedIn. But first, an admission: Over the years, I've been horrible at staying in touch with people. It's not because of no interest – it's because of no time. But now, I no longer have any excuse. And, neither do you.

Now, for instance, when you have significant change in your life or career, a new assignment, a job change to a new location, an award you've just received, or a new baby, or you've just divorced and you want to get back in circulation (hey, just kidding!), you can use LinkedIn to notify your contacts by making a simple update to your profile. All it takes is thirty seconds to do this and all your contacts are instantly updated.

And if you want to reach out, you can do this too with a follow-up email message to your contacts saying "I would love to catch up with you to give you the scoop on what's happening – call me when you get a chance at (xxx) xxx-xxxx!" It's that keeping-up process that sparks conversations, keeps your relationships fresh and will enhance your career and your life.

So, there you have it, my 15 amazing, sneaky little ways you can use LinkedIn to advance your HR career.

You should try to spend at least 30 minutes per week managing your LinkedIn presence. If you do that, I believe you'll find that it will pay off well for you in the future.

Unwritten HR Rule #9

Optimize your use of LinkedIn. As an HR professional, it's the best online tool you can use to keep your resume up to date, stay in touch with your network, search for jobs, prepare for interviews and market yourself.

Part Two

HOW TO ATTRACT THE BEST HR CAREER OPPORTUNITIES TO YOUR DOORSTEP

10

THE P.O.W.E.R. FORMULA FOR MAKING THE BEST HR JOBS COME TO YOU

As I revealed in Chapter 1, Inland Steel applied a painful, but important kick to my behind that forced me to recognize that becoming visible and generating buzz about what you're doing is a crucial strategy in taking your HR career to the next level. It will not only help you within your company, but it can also attract HR jobs in other organizations to you as well.

Let me explain.

Most HR people hate the job search process. I don't mean finding candidates for jobs. I mean finding jobs for themselves! Consequently, many HR folks are reluctant to put themselves on the job market -- even when they should. They fear the rejection and frustration that searching for a new job entails. We have all heard the horror stories of job candidates who submit resumes for hundreds of "open jobs" and do not get one single, stinking response back. Or others who have been told to network and make 50 new contacts a week just to get one interview that never pans out.

As a result of these frustrations, many HR folks decide it's just easier to stay put and look for new opportunities only when they've gotten laid off, fired, or have been passed over for a promotion for the fifth time.

Thankfully, I've never been laid off and forced to look for a job. I've been fortunate that by using just a couple of the techniques I'm about to share with you, I've been able to attract -- and not seek out -- new assignments, promotions and opportunities throughout my career while enjoying the luxury of remaining in the best city on earth...Chicago.

If I had to look for an HR job today, I'd go crazy. To me, there's no worse way to spend time than by trying to convince someone that I'm the best candidate for the job in an interview – someone who doesn't know me, has never heard of me, or may have someone else in mind for the job.

So, I'm here to tell you: I DON'T think you should ever put yourself in a position where you're beating the bushes for *any* human resources position.

What you should do instead is to focus on positioning yourself so that great, exciting organizations seek you out in order to obtain your services. You want the great HR jobs to chase you, not the other way around.

Here's How 70% of HR Jobs Are Filled – No Matter What You've Been Told!

The HR job market is like the rest of the job market. About 70% of the HR jobs are never advertised. They are part of the "hidden job market." These jobs go to those on the "inside track" -- someone who has already been anointed or pre-selected. That someone is a known quantity and someone recognizable. Chances are this person has been established as the lead candidate for the job through the company's annual talent review process, succession planning meetings or through personal or work relationships. **So, if you want to move up in your organization, you have to become that person.**

Even if your company has a job posting process where all jobs up to a certain level are publicized, it doesn't matter. In many cases, there is typically a "preferred candidate" who knows about the position in advance and has been informally vetted while the job is still hidden and unpublicized.

With these types of "hidden" opportunities there is no way for you to find them. They must find you. And the only way that will happen is by making yourself visible inside and outside of your organization so that you become the HR candidate of choice. If you do this right way, you can become so appealing that your current employer (or a new one) may pull out all the stops and create position just for you.

The P.O.W.E.R. Formula For Tapping Into The Hidden HR Job Market – And Making Great Opportunities Come To You

There are a variety of ways to do this, but there are five that work best:

- Public Speaking in your HR area of expertise.
- Organization Leadership and not waiting on direction.
- Writing proactively online and offline.
- Everyday Meetings: using them to enhance your impact.
- Representing Your Company and volunteering.

I call this my P.O.W.E.R. formula for making great HR jobs come to you. In the next five chapters, I'll take each element of this formula, break it down in detail and describe how you can apply each one.

<u>Unwritten HR Rule #10</u>

To make the best HR jobs come to you, follow the P.O.W.E.R. formula to tap into the hidden job market. This formula involves:
<u>P</u>ublic Speaking
<u>O</u>rganization Leadership
<u>W</u>riting Proactively
<u>E</u>veryday Meetings
<u>R</u>epresenting Your Company

11

SPEAK OUT ON YOUR HR SPECIALTY

Public speaking and giving talks in your HR area of expertise is one of the fastest ways to attract favorable attention from those who can help advance your human resources career.

As stated earlier, public speaking represents the "P" in the P.O.W.E.R. formula.

Speaking gives you tremendous visibility and credibility by giving you an avenue to put your confidence, your mastery of an HR topic and your communications skills on display.

The more you speak, the more your reputation and credibility increases. Gradually you'll become recognized as the expert on your subject. You'll become sought after for your opinions. And, over time, you'll find that career opportunities will begin to find their way to you because of your increased visibility.

There are a variety of different avenues for you to speak. You can:

- Speak at your company's orientation program for new employees.
- Present at your business or department's annual or quarterly meetings.

- Farm yourself out to other divisions within your company to speak at their meetings as an expert in one of your division's "best practices."
- Present at local or national HR industry conferences.
- Participate on panels and concurrent sessions at large HR conferences or business meetings.
- Present to local civic and community groups.
- Speak up more frequently in regularly scheduled meetings with your team or with your colleagues

One of the best things I ever did for my career in HR was becoming a good public speaker. Notice I said good, not great! I'm no Barack Obama or Tony Robbins. My biggest asset is simply a willingness to step up to the podium and share my message – I guess because so many people chose not to or will not do it.

Let me share three personal examples that demonstrate the power of public speaking.

Speaking On Campus To College Students
About Personal, Real-Life HR Experiences

Earlier in my career after I got my first HR job, I would return to campus and give talks to undergraduate and graduate students. My topic was: How to get your first HR job and survive in corporate America in your first few years. This was probably the only thing I could have spoken on at the time. I gave these talks at: University of Illinois, Michigan State, University of Wisconsin, Purdue, Atlanta University, Emory University, Indiana University, Calumet College, and Purdue-Calumet.

The fact that I was still at an age where I could still be mistaken for a college student myself (which is certainly not the case now!), made my talks go over especially well. All I did was simply tell my story, describe my HR experiences and offer tips based on what I'd learned.

Over the years, as a result of these talks, professors and placement office administrators I met during my visits passed on job leads to me of companies looking for experienced HR candidates. I must have received at least 12-15 invitations to interview for jobs that would never have happened otherwise because of speaking to these groups on campus.

No matter who you are and how much (or how little) HR experience you have, there are always people a few steps behind you in your career that can learn from your examples and experiences. You'll also find that college professors are happy to have some of their workload relieved by having a guest speaker come in to share real world experiences – especially a former alumnus. It's easy to get these speaking engagements because there are lots of potential professors to approach.

Moonlighting As An Evening Instructor
Teaching Human Resources Classes

The second experience occurred at about the same time. While working full time as an HR generalist at Inland, I also taught evening classes in Human Resources at a few local universities. At different times, I taught at Indiana University (Northwest campus), Purdue University (Calumet campus) and Calumet College. From a professional standpoint, this helped me polish my speaking skills, boosted my confidence, and gave me exposure to an entirely new set of acquaintances. It also put a few extra bucks in my pocket too, though that wasn't the main goal.

Again, this exposure led to referrals to headhunters who, because of my newfound visibility, began calling me about very attractive, corporate HR opportunities that again I would have never, ever heard about otherwise.

In some cases, I would return phone calls to these recruiters with names of colleagues as referrals. By helping them out, a couple of these headhunters became lifelong friends. As a result, I was supremely confident that if I ever needed to jump ship for another, better HR opportunity, my personal rolodex of headhunter contacts could deliver for me.

Local universities, their extension programs and seminar providers are always looking for guest lecturers, instructors and part-time faculty members who have real-life, in the trenches work experience they can draw from. You never know who is in your classroom and who knows whom.

Delivering In-House Seminars, Conferences And Workshops

The third experience had the single biggest impact on my HR career progression. I spent five years as a manager in Quaker's human resources development group. This group was headed by Mike Cohen, who I introduced you to in Chapter 5. Mike's group was highly respected in our organization and accountable for all the in-house leadership and talent development training, which was significant. As one of the stand-up trainers in the group, I was responsible for delivering workshops and seminars aimed at middle and senior managers. These programs covered areas such as: managing performance, coaching employees, giving feedback, selling ideas, change management and teamwork. In all, I've calculated that over 3000 managers went through training sessions that I conducted either solo or in partnership with other trainers during the time.

As a trainer, you are positioned as the expert to your attendees. And, I'd often have managers and executives as participants in my sessions who were two to three levels above me in the organization. They were in a great position to observe how I communicated, engaged the group in discussions, and answered tough questions while leading a meeting. In many ways it was like auditioning for a promotion every time you did a session. In addition, because these programs often lasted 3-4 days at remote offsite locations, we shared meals, breaks and evening activities that allowed personal rapport building and bonding to occur with these leaders that could have never happened back on the job. Yes, we even closed down a few bars. A few more than I can count.

Today, I directly attribute three promotions I received in HR to the exposure and relationships I built with leaders who went through these training sessions. In a couple of cases, very senior line managers went to bat for me as their preferred candidate to fill an executive HR role working directly with their organizations. And they based their opinion largely on our shared training experience together. They got to know me on a personal basis, know my work having observed it first hand during training and were comfortable with me. Their endorsements gave me a tremendous leverage when my credentials were weighed against those of other HR candidates for these same positions.

I don't share all these speaking experiences to brag. But instead to demonstrate the awesome power that public speaking can provide in making connections and building relationships which can attract HR job opportunities to you.

Four Additional Insights About Public Speaking As A Career Advancement Strategy

#1: Aspiring senior HR leaders look for opportunities to speak all the time. If you want to be noticed and someday reach the most senior HR level, seek out any and all opportunities to speak. Senior HR leaders speak up at meetings. They give updates frequently. They participate in team presentations to employee groups. They address business teams and professional associations. If you're just getting started as a speaker, start small. Begin with "lunch and learn" meetings in your company, then move on to large conference room sessions and then on to larger quarterly business meetings or professional organization meetings. Offer to put together a panel and serve as a moderator. Take it step by step, but seize every opportunity to speak -- even if it makes you nervous at first. The more you speak, the more comfortable you'll become sharing your ideas. As your experience increases, you'll develop greater confidence, while others will develop greater respect for you and your abilities.

#2: If you have stage fright or lack confidence in speaking, join Toastmasters. Toastmaster groups are everywhere and are highly recommended by everyone. They give you a chance to give small practice talks and get advice and feedback from other people. You also get to see role models. Like everything else, you'll find that your speaking will improve with practice. But here's a twist: Don't join the Toastmasters inside of your organization. Go to one a few miles away or to the nearest big city if you can. This allows you to polish up your speaking skills, make mistakes, and boost your confidence out of sight of people in your organization. It also allows you to network and build relationships with a different circle of acquaintances that may have potential career connections you might later capitalize on.

#3: Develop your own unique presentation "road show." This is another terrific public speaking strategy. It involves developing your own canned presentation that you can deliver to different audiences. It can be based on a project you've completed, a best practice you're very familiar with or your own HR experience. You then develop a 45-60 minute presentation for it, slap a fancy title on it and then look for opportunities to deliver this talk anytime you can. This presentation enables you to raise your visibility and promote your expertise inside and outside of your organization to different groups at a moment's notice.

It allows you to say to potential meeting planners, who are always looking for interesting speakers: "Listen, I've got a 45 to 60 minute presentation on performance appraisals that's fun, funny and will help your team as they're preparing for the upcoming review cycle."

The title you give your presentation is <u>critical.</u> The title should be selected before you go out and speak. It acts like a headline. Don't take this step lightly, because if you give it a lousy title, nobody will want to come hear what you have to say, even if you're providing valuable information. People don't want to be bored. So take the time to craft an interesting title.

Here are some example titles you might consider adapting to your topic:

- *Best Practices For Conducting Easy & Painless Performance Reviews*
- *10 Low-Cost, High Impact Strategies For Building Your Team*
- *How To Use Our Compensation Program To Build Your Personal Wealth*
- *Critical Facts About Labor Contracts That All Front Line Leaders Must Know*
- *11 Strategies For Keeping Your Best People – Before It's Too Late!*
- *15 Ways To Keep Your Location (or Department) Union-Free*
- *Secrets For Assessing & Picking The Best Candidates In Interviews*

Be specific in your title. Titles that begin *"How To...,"* *"13 Ways To...,"* *"7 Strategies For...,"* or the like usually work best. Not only do they tell your audience exactly what you're going to teach them, but it adds a ton of specificity and credibility to your presentation. People generally respond favorably to specifics much more than generalities.

#4: Don't think you have to be a Zig Ziglar, Jesse Jackson or some sort of spell binding motivational speaker to be a successful speaker. You just have to be clear, passionate about your topic and informative. Your colleagues (or potential hiring managers in the audience) just want to know what you know and be a little entertained in the process. So, just get out there and start sharing what you know. If you provide information that is useful, spice it up with personal stories and keep your presentation simple, your name will get around and you'll be flooded with e-mails and phone messages with new speaking opportunities.

At some point in your career, speaking well could be the single factor that determines your success in HR. If your career feels stalled, the reason may be the way you are communicating with your important audiences. You may not be able to break through the ceiling to the big HR jobs until you know how to articulate your ideas fluidly and confidently. Public speaking is the pathway that can provide that for you.

Unwritten HR Rule #11

Speaking and giving presentations in your HR area of expertise is one of the fastest ways to attract favorable attention from those who can help advance your human resources career. Speaking gives you tremendous visibility and credibility by giving you an avenue to put your confidence, your mastery of an HR topic and your communications skills on display.

12

LEADING & NOT WAITING ON DIRECTION

Organization leadership represents the "O" in the P.O.W.E.R. formula.

Stepping in and assuming the mantle of organization leadership when the situation calls for it is an awesome way of setting yourself apart from the rest of the HR pack and attracting HR opportunities.

Let me give you an example by describing...

How Lori Turned Her Frustration With Her Manager Into An Organization Leadership Opportunity And Her Next Promotion In HR

Lori was an HR manager in our Quaker Oats Food Service Division and was an attendee at one of our annual HR National meetings. She was there with her boss and a number of her HR colleagues.

During a break in the meeting, she cornered me and asked: "Could I talk to you alone for a minute?" So she and I ducked out of the meeting room, went down the hall, and found an empty meeting room to step into.

"I am very, very frustrated," she told me.

"There are so many things we could be doing with our clients to move the business forward. We keep hearing about all these new HR best practices that all the other divisions are doing, but my boss never gets anything new implemented. Nothing happens. Our team knows that when he comes back from a big meeting like this and talks about all the new things other HR teams are doing, all we have to do is wait a few days and it'll all blow over."

"What kinds of things would you have him do?" I asked.

"Run some webinars for our managers on how to use our performance management system better, create an on-boarding program for our new hires, and do some retention risk assessments of our key talent to determine what we need to do to keep them. Also many of the other divisions have started looking into programs to address work life balance issues for working moms. We haven't done anything."

"Wait a minute," I said, raising my hand like a traffic cop and bringing her to a halt. "Lori, these all sound like excellent ideas to me and most don't require any senior management approval to implement. Right?"

"Right. But he won't do any of them," she said sadly.

"Well, Lori," I said, "*what are YOU waiting for?*"

For the first time that day, Lori was speechless. We didn't have time to continue our discussion so she returned to the meeting room with a dazed, but thoughtful look on her face.

You see, it's easy to complain about your manager's failure to take charge, pick up the ball and just run with it. And in this case, Lori was certainly justified in being frustrated by her boss's lack of initiative.

She told me she had complained to him and about him for over a year. And, she had been frustrated all that time.

Obviously, that wasn't going to change anything. So to me, her options were obvious.

One, accept him and the situation and stop being perturbed.

Two, continue to complain and feel frustrated every day as long as she reported to him.

Three, leave this job and this manager.

And four, take charge, demonstrate organization leadership and get some of these things going herself.

A lot of HR folks I've talked with would have chosen to accept the situation and take out their frustrations by either suffering in silence or continuing to complain.

A few would even try and sabotage their manager, which inevitably could backfire on them.

Not Lori.

About a year later, Lori and I connected again at another one of our division HR meetings. The night before, her manager -- the one that she had a problem with a year before -- privately raved about Lori to me over dinner and disclosed that he was planning to promote her.

The next day, Lori cornered me again on a break away from her manager. "I want to tell you," she began, "that I was very angry with you and the way you answered me that day. I wanted some sympathy. And frankly, I wanted you to go have a talk with my manager. But I sure didn't want you to challenge me."

"Should I apologize?" I asked.

"Not at all," she answered.

"Let me tell you about what's happened in the last year. I started running 'Performance Management & Leadership,' training sessions and have taken over fifty managers through this program. It covers writing objectives, coaching employees, and doing end-of-year performance reviews. Our managers are thrilled with the sessions. I worked with our OD people to develop a new on-boarding program for our new hourly hires which has already begun to decrease our turnover rate. I contacted one of our sister divisions and they agreed to not only share their work life program with us but they've helped us put on some lunch and learn sessions with our working moms on work life balance."

"I'm excited about what we've accomplished. I'm through waiting for things to happen. I'm now taking charge."

**Three Important Insights About Demonstrating
Organization Leadership To Advance Your Career**

#1: Great HR leadership is not about waiting for direction. It's about stepping in and providing direction. Look around you. What things are frustrating you? Make a list of these things and what you could do to take action now to resolve them. You'll find that there's a leadership vacuum practically everywhere. If you're overwhelmed with choices, choose the highest priority item and force yourself to make the time. Create a plan to accomplish your objective and share it with your manager. Start with baby steps. You'll be shocked at how great it makes you feel – not to mention those around you. Use the positive response you receive to spur you on to taking even greater initiative in the future.

#2: Look for HR leadership opportunities after layoffs have occurred. Lots of times, after layoffs, there's a kind of ghoulish rummaging for the leftovers: newly vacant offices, the nicer furniture, even blackberries, phones and staplers. Don't focus your attention on these things.

If you've survived the layoffs yourself, figure out what your company may have lost in the ax-wielding and step in to provide it. For example, if your organization has cut the training and development staff, can you step in and offer to deliver a portion of that training? Since you're not an expert, the expectations may be low and the organization may be appreciative of providing any sort of continuity in these services.

Many times, during layoffs, companies get rid of HR specialists who were "nice to have" during boom times but become too costly to keep when it comes to pinching pennies. Can you step in and replace part of the skill set that just went out the door? If you can, do it.

#3: Piggyback on new, emerging initiatives in your organization. Can you provide HR leadership and support for groups that are working on new, leading edge initiatives in your organization like environmental sustainability, green technologies, clean energy, or how to best leverage online social media.

These groups tend to have very small budgets and little HR support. If you can be the HR person that can step in and help these groups think through the staffing, talent, compensation, change management or people implications of their decisions, you can become a hero and add tremendous value to your organization. But it's your job to take the initiative, build the bridge to these groups and make your case.

Extra Bonus Tip! Step in and offer to lead the continuing education initiative for a specific group (e.g. Finance or HR) or for your entire company. This is a huge void in most organizations. As the continuing education czar, you meet with individuals and monitor the certifications and training seminars that can enhance performance. You benchmark your in-house training programs with those of other companies in your industry. You look for new, cost-effective cutting-edge programs that can enhance performance. You bring in outside speakers and programs that can provide fresh ideas to enhance the group or company's competitiveness. By offering to bring accountability, organization and enhanced ROI for this entire initiative, you can deliver great value to your organization and improved visibility for yourself.

Unwritten HR Rule #12

There are HR leadership voids practically everywhere if you look for them. Stepping into these situations and taking charge is a great way of setting yourself apart from the rest of the HR pack.

13

WRITING PROACTIVELY TO ADVANCE YOUR HR CAREER

Writing proactively is the "W" in the P.OW.E.R. formula.

Being able to put your ideas down on paper is a powerful way to help others discover you. The way you express yourself in your written or electronic communications carries your name and reputation to people who might never learn of you otherwise.

No matter how much HR experience you have, if you have a point of view and opinion that other HR people enjoy reading about, you will stand out and greatly benefit from the effort to get your words in print. Once you've written something, it's not unusual to have people who don't know you to contact you and say, "Wow, I just read what you wrote the other day and I thought it was great, and I'd like to talk to you more about it!"

There are a number of ways you can help your HR career with your writing skills:

Volunteering to be your busy boss' ghostwriter on memos, reports and presentations. If you can compose messages with impact or put together graphically persuasive Power Point presentation decks, your overworked boss and even her boss will seek your assistance to lighten the load with their projects.

Preparing reports on new opportunities you've discovered. Taking the initiative to spot an emerging HR trend and then writing up a report about it…including a recommended action or proposal…can brand you as a thought leader within your organization.

Submitting regular executive summaries or progress updates on long-term projects. On HR initiatives that span six months or longer, keeping the boss aware of how the project is progressing through frequent written updates will label you as someone who has your boss' back. However, doing data dumps isn't your goal here. Instead, you want to prepare brief, bulleted reports, citing progress made, any danger signals and your recommended remedies.

Thanking your way to success. Sending thank you notes to lift up morale, stroke your boss or congratulate a colleague is like a written pat on the back. You can win friends and gain attention with personal handwritten notes sent at the right time, which in today's email-based culture, has practically gone out of style. Send notes to anyone in your office who's been recognized for anything – a promotion, an employee of the month award, or for a job well done. A few lines of sincere and heartfelt congratulations will enable you to stand out and your thoughtfulness is remembered. *Caution:* Don't overload people by sending too many memos. This is like talking too much during staff meetings. Pretty soon people stop paying attention and your words lose their impact. Conserve your memos for a specific purpose, not to advertise your existence.

Writing articles to expand your reputation outside of your organization. Candidly, getting an article published in widely read industry journals such as *HR Executive* or *Workforce* is not that easy. However, don't let that worry you. While it doesn't hurt to try, you don't have to be published in these slick trade magazines to get your name out. You can start with letters to the editor of these magazines, or articles for your company's blog, or articles that you write for a LinkedIn group you belong to. Newsletters and websites of your local HR association chapters are also always seeking thoughtful insights from their professional members. Contact the committee chairs and brainstorm some of your ideas with them. Make sure you convey the point that your insights are not based on theory, but come from your real life experiences in the HR trenches. Articles such as these allow you to build your reputation as an opinion leader that commands respect.

Launching your own HR blog. If you don't already have a blog, stop reading this book and go start one right this minute. If you need inspiration, check out HR blogs by:

Kris Dunn, (HRCapitalist.com)
Michael Haberman, (OmegaHRSolutions.blogspot.com),
Lisa Rosendahl (HRManager.squarespace.com)
Lance Haum (YourHRGuy.com)
Angelique Kennedy (InspiredHR.blogspot.com).

Your blog is your living resume. It shows how you think and how you write. It shows what's important to you. It can draw career or entrepreneurial opportunities to you that you would not believe.

What's your HR passion? It is Compensation Design? Leadership Development? Labor Negotiations? Resume Writing? Diversity Programs? Educate us on your passion and help us grow through your blog. Blogs are relatively easy and cheap to set up. And, they give you an instant publishing platform to discuss hot issues in your niche. They're an excellent way to brand yourself as a go-to source for current information, news, and your opinions.

Employers of the future will love bloggers. Microsoft and Apple love 'em now – they're ahead of the curve and they get it. Frankly, other companies haven't caught on – at least, not yet. Bloggers are mentors. And employers love hiring mentors because they raise everyone's performance. One caveat, this does not give you the right to be a raging lunatic on your blog (sometimes how I fear I come off sometimes on my own blog at SuccessInHR.com). But it is the chance for you to show off what you're capable of doing, what you've done, and what you can do for others who can really benefit from your expertise.

Partnering with a consultant you've worked with. Consultants are always looking for ways to get more publicity, elevate their image, attract more customers and generate more revenue for their consulting practice. If you're working with a consultant on a breakthrough project in your organization, why not propose teaming up on an article that shares both of your perspectives. If you've not written an article before, partnering with someone with experience is a lot better than going solo. Another great advantage is that the consultant may already have built-in connections with magazine editors or publishing contacts that can help get the article published.

Collaborating with your corporate communications department. This group is constantly looking for positive stories about your organization. They also tend to always be on deadline and understaffed. So your help in writing a story or article for publication would be welcomed. You will be helping them achieve their objective of getting exposure and publicity for your company. Typically, they are experienced in working with novice writers. So, they may be very happy to edit what you've written to make it look even better when published.

Publishing a white paper, special report or book on your expertise. A sure-fire way to establish yourself as an expert and enhance your reputation is to write a book. Being a published author is very powerful. In the minds of most people, it directly catapults you into expert status. Even people, who have never heard of you, will put you on a pedestal because you've been published.

However, writing a book won't provide an immediate boost to your career since it will take you months (and maybe even years) to complete a high quality book on your HR topic. And therefore, this may not be the best route to take especially if you're holding down a full-time job and looking for a jolt in your HR career now.

But a more immediate strategy is to publish white papers or special reports. And, I am a direct example of this strategy.

Before publishing this book, I authored the *"HR Recession Guide: 7 Ways To Recession Proof Your HR Career & Avoid Losing Your Job."* If you don't have a copy, it's available as free downloadable PDF at www.HRRecessionGuide.com. This 20 page special report took me about a week to put together, working just evenings. It was downloaded 462 times within the first eight days it was released and has now been downloaded well over 2000 times. All I did to publicize it was to email my HR network about it and post a few comments on LinkedIn with a link back to where this report could be accessed. And, through the magic of the internet and viral marketing, it spread like wildfire. The result: after being a relative unknown outside of my company, this report has helped brand me nationally as an authority on "HR career advancement" in less than 60 days. Also, as a result of this one simple report alone, I've been able to attract publishing companies, recruiters with open senior executive HR jobs, speaking engagements, one-on-one paid coaching requests and entrepreneurs interested in partnering on potentially lucrative HR-related opportunities. You can too.

Another example of someone who has used the special report or white paper approach successfully is Sandy Jones-Kaminski. Sandy is the author of *"12 Rules of Networking for HR Professionals."* Her white paper is about 20 pages long and she's made it available as a free download at www.BellaDomain.com. In fact, it is so good that I contacted her and got her permission to include it as Chapter 20 in this book, crediting her fully as the author. In addition to providing great information to you, it provides wonderful increased exposure to Sandy by bringing her name and capabilities to the thousands in HR that will read this book. You can do the same thing. Think about the type of HR special report or white paper you could author and the possibilities that it might have for providing positive publicity for your HR career.

Extra Bonus Tip!   LinkedIn allows you upload PowerPoint presentations to include as part of your personal profile. Why not take advantage of this and let employers see how brilliant you are? Here's how: Write out an 8-slide presentation that showcases your HR skills and expertise. Then, upload it to your LinkedIn profile. Passively, this presentation can be found online by headhunters, recruiters and employers, which is what you want. Actively, you can ask hiring managers to view your PowerPoint during a phone interview. Imagine the impact of saying, "Ms. Hiring Manager, if you're online, would you have a minute to view a presentation I created for our phone interview? It's called, '*7 Ways To XYZ Company Can Save Workforce and Human Resources Costs in the Next 90 Days.*'"   Think you don't have time for this? Think again. If you're in the HR job market, and have been looking for work 8-10 hours a day, why not take 3 hours a week from activities that aren't producing results -- like applying for advertised HR jobs online, for example -- and try this research method for a couple of weeks instead.

Unwritten HR Rule #13

Writing is a powerful way to help others discover you. No matter how much (or how little) experience you have, the way your words come across on paper or electronically carries your name and reputation to people who might never learn of you otherwise.

14

HOW TO SHOW UP STRONG AT EVERYDAY MEETINGS

The "E" in the P.O.W.E.R. formula stands for Everyday meetings.

Regularly contributing your ideas during everyday meetings is a great way to get noticed. In most organizations, it's a well known fact that if you attend a lot of meetings, say nothing and let others do all the talking you're labeled as someone lacking leadership potential. And, that my friend, can be the kiss of death for your career.

In fact, right or wrong, the research has found that...

Four Out Of Five Managers Evaluate Each Other Based On Their Meeting Behavior. And 87% Judge Leadership Based On How A Person Participates In A Meeting.

I hated meetings -- whether it was a staff meeting my boss conducted, monthly business meetings my business leader led, or project update meetings on key HR initiatives. It didn't matter.

I'm an introvert. I'd much rather e-mail, write this book, give a prepared presentation, or deal one-on-one rather than attend an everyday meeting.

Most times I had nothing against the meeting leader, but my experience was that most meetings just wasted my time. They were often unplanned, unproductive, unnecessary, unpleasant or just about any other "un-" you can think of. They weren't well managed or facilitated. They were tough places to get heard. Lots of voices competed for the floor. And, because my style was more laid back, I often had difficulty getting my points across, especially if I didn't do my homework to prepare beforehand.

But guess what...

Madonna Has A Better Chance Of Becoming A Virgin Than Meetings Have Of Ever Going Away

Love them or not, everyday meetings are a part of doing business. Not only are they important, they are *critical*. Whether they are effective or not, it is how consensus decisions are made and alignment is reached with diverse groups of people with different agendas.

So, meetings are a fact of life. I had to deal with them. And so do you. Therefore, you need to know how to show up strong in meetings and here are my recommendations:

Do your homework and plan in advance how you will contribute to the meeting. Some people don't take time to do homework before the meeting. Just by being prepared beforehand will give you a tremendous advantage. Know what the meeting is all about, the stated purpose as well as the hidden agenda. If you don't know, ask. Study the background materials. Set your own goal for the session. Make a list of two or three points, opinions, questions or insights in advance that you want to contribute to the discussion and compile the facts to support them. Obviously you don't want to just speak for the sake of speaking, but if you have something to say, prepare it in advance.

Be punctual – even if everyone else isn't. One of my earliest HR SVPs said that there were only two good reasons for being late for a meeting with her: one, you're dead; two, you want to be. If she had enforced this policy, we would have conducted all of our meetings at the local morgue. Sadly, she is not alone as most meetings don't start promptly and attendees become conditioned to arriving late. Don't fall into this trap, even if everyone else does. If you're late, and others have started without you, you begin at a disadvantage – and many times it's hard to catch up. You can be thrown off your game if the meeting has already started and you're operating in one stage while everyone else is in another.

Find something to contribute early. This will enable you to be seen as an independent thinking leader versus a second banana who always agrees with ideas already made. An easy way to score points in meetings is to jump in and ask questions to clarify the purpose of the meeting or the order of the agenda – especially if there have been agenda changes or there isn't an agenda at all, which happens frequently. This helps keep things on track and gets your voice heard early.

Offer your own ideas with confidence – but be prepared for push backs. As you present your views, ready yourself for your ideas to be challenged. However, don't take these disagreements personally. View them as simply cues that you need to provide additional facts or evidence that your idea is a good one. Resistance is natural. Sometimes it's legitimate. Most of the time, it's just human nature. Often others may disagree with your idea simply because they didn't understand it. When this happens, simply say, "I'm sorry I didn't make myself clear. What I was suggesting was..." Other times the resistance may be because someone flat out disagrees with your perspective. You should anticipate this. If your ideas are sound, don't backpedal or wimp out just to avoid conflict. You don't want a reputation as someone with no backbone that wilts under fire. Stand firm by reiterating your idea's benefits and how it contributes squarely to the issue being discussed. However, if the facts and evidence are not on your side, don't be resistant just to show that you can be. That's not leadership, that's being a jerk.

Have one "out-of-the-box" idea per meeting. This is your ace in the hole. Now, let me be clear: this shouldn't be an off-the-wall thought or something out of the clear blue sky unrelated to the topic under discussion. But rather it should be an idea you're sure your HR colleagues haven't thought of that's clearly aligned to the meeting topic. Thinking outside the box and demonstrating breakthrough thinking are qualities that many HR senior leaders admire and using meetings to show that you have them is a great strategy for demonstrating leadership. However, many HR professionals I've talked to are gun-shy about doing this for fear of looking foolish. To minimize this risk:

- Take your idea through your own mental interrogation process until you can clearly state in a few sentences what your idea is, why you hold it and what benefits it provides.
- Bounce your idea off of a trusted colleague or your mentor before the meeting. Have this person role play a typical response so you can anticipate likely objections.
- If you don't have time to fully bake your idea before the meeting, you can still offer it with confidence with some up-front disclaimers like: *"I've not completely fleshed this idea out, but..."* or the ever-popular *"Here is an out-of-the-box thought, what if we were to...."* or, *"This may seem far-fetched, but how about..."* The latter is my least favorite and should only be used if you exhausted all of the other disclaimers in your personal arsenal.

During the meeting, watch the tone of your questions. Thoughtful, well-timed questions are a brilliant way of contributing to a meeting, but be careful how you ask them. Questions are great, but showing up the presenter is not. Don't make the mistake of using this time as an opportunity to grandstand. If you wish to ask a legitimate question that has the potential to make the presenter look bad, ask it in a non-accusatory fashion.

For example, if the presenter opens the floor for questions without addressing a very basic issue that really should have been covered, the question you ask could make the person look stupid and make you look like a bastard. Be more professional than that. In order to lessen the blow, try prefacing your question with: *"Judy, I may have missed the answer to this, but could you explain..."* Doing this gives Judy an out. Your suggestion that you could have missed what she said positions your question constructively and implies that others may have missed it too.

Be positive, push back when necessary, but avoid killer statements. Challenging ideas and pushing back in meetings are important qualities to demonstrate. It adds to your credibility by showing that as an HR professional you can be edgy, assertive and strong. However, in showing this strength, don't go overboard. Repeated comments in meetings such as: *"We tried that three years ago and it didn't work..."* or *"The sales VPs will never go for that one..."* can backfire and build your reputation as someone that kills ideas all the time and is not a team player. You might also find yourself occasionally left off the invitation list for key meetings. So watch it. But at the same time, let me be clear. If you disagree with someone else's idea, express it and stand firm. However, make every attempt to balance your criticisms with solutions. No one likes the participant that knocks down every idea, but has none of their own. Although, disagreements are never pleasant, the meeting will be a complete waste of time if honest differences of opinion aren't discussed.

If you find yourself without anything to say, look for opportunities to build on the ideas of others. You don't have to, or shouldn't comment on every topic. Save your remarks for times when they can have real impact. However, if you're stuck in a meeting without any new ideas or provocative questions to contribute, the easiest way to show leadership is by adding to or strengthening an important point already made. This requires that you listen carefully to the views expressed before you jump in and not parrot what has been already been said. For example, you might chime in and say: *"I really like what Tina just mentioned about outsourcing our hourly hiring process. I believe it will free us up to spend more time being strategic business partners with the plant managers and will help us address their recent feedback about our lack of availability. Tina, would you agree?"* Or you might say: *"Tom's suggestion about having fewer 360 survey questions is a good one. There are three coaching questions that I believe we could drop without much trouble and I'd be delighted to work with Tom to identify others should we decide to go down this route..."* I can't emphasize enough that building on others' ideas, when done at the right time is an excellent reputation builder. It shows that you're analytical, supportive and engaged. Often, this can help you win fans among your colleagues and become sought out by the higher-ups for your "can-do" approach.

Develop post-meeting summaries and proposals. If your boss doesn't recap meeting results and assignments, volunteer to prepare them yourself for the team from your agenda notes in a succinct form, ready for your boss' sign off. If an idea came up that you weren't ready to talk about during the meeting, think it through, briefly outline your plan, and have it on your boss' desk by the next morning. Or, if you expressed an idea at the meeting for which the boss wanted more background, provide a written summary with specific information...promptly.

Unwritten HR Rule #14

Don't underestimate the importance of everyday meetings. Showing up big and regularly contributing your ideas during meetings is a great way to get noticed and labels you as a strong leader and someone capable of assuming broader HR accountabilities.

15

THE AWESOME POWER OF REPRESENTING YOUR COMPANY EXTERNALLY

Representing your company at external events, conferences or meetings is the "R" in the P.O.W.E.R. formula.

This is yet another productive way of raising your professional profile and providing a different avenue for you to attract HR job opportunities.

For years, I was honored and humbled to represent Pepsi as a member of the Executive Leadership Council (ELC). ELC is one of the preeminent organizations for African-American business leaders in the world and comprises only the most senior African-American corporate executives in Fortune 500 companies.

I could have declined this honor and chosen one of the many human resources associations available locally or nationally as Pepsi's representative. But I felt ELC was a better match with my own personal goals and objectives.

By representing my division of Pepsi at quarterly conferences with this organization, I got a regular dose of exposure to this gathering of senior executive leaders that would never have occurred if I was just back at my desk just shooting the breeze. I made lots of business contacts, which later resulted in being invited to explore a couple of unpublicized HR executive job opportunities, even though I was not actively on the job market.

This is the benefit that you too can gain by representing your company externally. The key is to choose (or get selected for) organizations, meetings or conferences which have objectives connected to yours, have members with whom you wish to associate, and can provide you with opportunities to network like crazy.

If you make a point of extracting every bit of value out of the experience, you'll go home with pockets full of business cards, key contacts and relationships which could lead to lucrative HR opportunities down the road.

You generally score points just by being *available* to attend these outside organization meetings and conferences in the first place. Usually, the most senior HR leaders don't have time to go, unless they're featured speakers or it's being held in some exotic location. They prefer instead to send more junior HR folks to represent the company and bring back the goodies. The goodies aren't desk paperweights emblazoned with the conference logo, it is information about what's going on in your industry -- new HR insights or industry best practices you can share with the team (or interesting tidbits, rumors or gossip).

From a career standpoint, your number-one job when representing your company at a conference or meeting is to be a great ambassador for your company, look sharp, act sharp....**and make connections.** Not the brainless business card-swapping kind, but the substantial kind that turns a new acquaintance into a lasting resource.

If you're representing your company at an HR conference for example, that personable HR director from Phoenix you talked to about designing employee incentive plans for thirty minutes at the opening dinner reception may be a valuable reference. Or even a future employer. But you'll never know that unless you make a good connection and follow up by staying in touch.

Here are three specific goals you should set for yourself when returning from an external conference or meeting:

- You should bring back at least *one useful insight* you can share with your colleagues within 72 hours of your arrival back.
- You should have made a least *one new, significant contact,* someone you can add right away to your LinkedIn network.
- And if your boss runs into someone who was also at that conference, that person should be able to say *you made a great impression and represented the company well.*

If you've accomplished these three things, consider your experience golden.

Here are some additional tips for capitalizing on conferences and external events as an envoy of your employer:

Dress above what's required. Now isn't the time to break out your Hawaiian shorts and flip-flops because you're at a seaside conference in Miami. Whatever the dress code is for the conference – which you can usually find in the registration materials – dress a couple of steps above it. Because you're going to be meeting people you don't know, go with business casual rather than grubby, weekend casual.

Resist the urge to leave early. Stay for the whole conference. Attend every social event. You don't have to stay until they turn out the lights at every dinner or party; just be sure to milk every chance to make an impression and connect. And try to stay in the hotel where the conference is held. It's easier to get to each event and solidify connections with people you meet because you'll run into them multiple times.

Stretch yourself socially and participate actively in conference discussions. Asking great questions during Q&A sessions is a first step towards raising your profile. Make certain you take advantage of the chance to introduce yourself to industry experts, conference coordinators and other attendees. Go out of your way to introduce yourself to anyone, everyone. If you can, offer to be a break-out facilitator, discussion moderator, or any opportunity to get involved. It's a good way to build your professional reputation and enhance your networking opportunities.

Share your business card and collect business cards. But remember: *It's not a contest of who can collect the most cards. The goal is to come home with one killer card – and for yours to be the killer card someone else takes back to his or her Rolodex.*

If this is a tradeshow, network with the trade show vendors. Don't be one of those attendees that races up and down the trade show isles with a shopping bag, avoiding eye contact with the exhibitors, and grabbing handfuls of useless junk. Stop and talk to the vendors, ask questions, be courteous, and represent your company in a professional way. Sure, help yourself to the goodies, just don't go overboard. And if you're extra nice, you may get one of the prime giveaways they hide under the table.

Bring home the goods. Write a short e-mail summary for your boss and other relevant parties summarizing takeaways or industry news. Offer to share any new best practices or innovative concepts with your team individually or at the next staff meeting. And before the conference shine fades, look for a way – immediately – to apply what you've learned back on the job. *And make sure your boss sees it happen.* Taking these actions will dramatically improve your payoff from the experience.

Finally, bring gifts back for your family or loved ones. These don't have to be expensive, but can be small, budget-friendly mementos that show that they've been in your thoughts while you've been gone.

Here Are Four Ways To Represent Your Company And Enhance Your Career At The Same Time

#1: Become your company's representative in local or national human resources associations. These are the organizations that you are no doubt already familiar with. Associations such as:

- Society for Human Resource Management (SHRM) and its hundreds of local chapters.
- International Personnel Management Association (IPMA).
- American Society of Training and Development (ASTD).
- Organization Development Network (ODN).

Because the programs offered by these associations allow you to beef up your competence in your current job, if you need to, make the case to your employer that they pay for all of the costs associated with your membership to these groups. But don't be just a member. Look for way to take a leadership role in one of these organizations. By doing so, you have the chance to impress people in your field of expertise. That could lead to a better job at another company. Committees are always looking for help, and almost any activity will help you meet new people, and give them a chance to get to know you. However, the best committees for truly networking among your peers and colleagues are the membership, program, and fund-raising committees. With these sub-groups, you meet current members, newcomers, and thought leaders who may speak before the monthly meetings. Try to introduce them at these gatherings. Every time you stand up in front of the assembled membership, that's a few more minutes for you in the spotlight. And, it's another opportunity for you to get noticed.

#2: Become the HR representative for your corporate communications department. Partner with your corporate communications department and offer your services in helping to put out the good word about what your company is doing. Make a list of the various HR initiatives that you're involved with that put your company in a positive light and set up time to review them with your corporate communications contact. Using this list as your foundation, volunteer to lead the project to apply for the various "Best Place To Work" lists that are published each year. Or volunteer to be on the list of employees cleared to speak with the press. Ask to be given media training so that you understand the rules and finer points of giving interviews. However, make sure all of this cleared with your boss beforehand.

#3: Assist your community affairs group. Most companies have a community affairs department. In most organizations, this department manages the company's huge charitable foundation. In some other companies, it is the conduit for employees looking for a way to give back to their communities. As a representative of HR, you can volunteer to organize and drive high visibility charitable events like United Way, Big Brother & Big Sister Programs, while engaging employees in good works for the community and society at large.

#4: Become an HR spokesman for your governmental affairs group. Step up to the plate and volunteer to speak out for your company on critical HR-related issues like employee rights to unionize, or immigration laws, or FMLA. It's important that you have passion for these issues and can talk about them credibly. You might find yourself describing the impacts of new bills before HR industry associations or your company's senior management team. You could eventually find yourself at your state capitol or in Washington D.C. lobbying for these issues at highest levels of our government. If you're not high enough in the HR food chain to become an appropriate spokesman on these issues, then support the HR person who is. Be that person's go-to contact operating behind the scenes, even if it means doing grunt work or collating documents. By being there, getting noticed, and learning the ropes from within, you gain valuable exposure.

If all this feels like a lot of work, you're right. It is. No doubt about it. However, I've seen careers of up and coming HR folks skyrocket as a result of stepping up and getting engaged in external affairs.

<u>Unwritten HR Rule #15</u>

Representing your company at external events, conferences, or meetings is a great way to raise your professional profile and provide an avenue for HR job opportunities to come to you.

Part Three

ENGAGING OTHER PEOPLE WHO WILL HELP YOU ADVANCE YOUR HR CAREER

16

CREATING YOUR G.R.A.N.D. NETWORK OF RELATIONSHIPS

Lone rangers don't travel far up the HR career ladder.

The higher you scale the HR food chain, the more you will require a network of trusted relationships. You can't possibly know everything you need to know to be successful – no one can.

The HR professionals and executives who are the most proactive in building their personal connections and alliances -- and utilize them to the max to provide feedback, coaching, and support -- are the ones who flourish.

Like you, I have plenty of relationships in my life. However, the ones that I can really open up to, share my fears, failures, goals and dreams with and ask for help are the most productive ones to me. They are people that can deliver the kind of insight and feedback that I need to hear most and they are worth their weight in gold.

When I became an HR leader, people looked at me as the expert. I was supposed to be the one with all the answers. Needless to say, I didn't always have them. When I came up against massive organization, professional and personal problems that were just too big to solve alone, I needed help. And that was the time I tapped into my circle of relationships. That's the time you should as well.

However, there are other alternatives, but none of them are as good as having your own network of relationships to draw on.

For example, you can hire a coach. And many people do. Executive coaching, career coaching, and life coaching comprise a $3 billion dollar market. And it's growing at a 25 percent a year clip. This profession fills a needed void that exists in the marketplace for candid, objective guidance and support. The only problem is that you have to spend thousands of dollars to get a coach and there's no guarantee that you'll find one that will provide what you need.

Online networking sites are another resource you can use, but they are not the complete answer either. LinkedIn, Facebook, Twitter...the list is endless...they're not enough. In *Who's Got Your Back*, Keith Ferrazzi puts it well: "You can talk about the fact that you have thousands of online 'friends' and 'contacts' but the average business professional doesn't have more than three of them that they can confide in on matters that are important, according to a study done in 2006 by the American Sociological Review. And since that original study, that number has now dropped to an average of two people – with more 25% of all Americans in business admitting they have NO confidents at all!"

So, you can't depend on online networking sites or paid coaches alone as your support network.

I believe the real path to HR success is through creating your own network of relationships, contacts and connections – with trusted individuals that will open doors and provide the kind of encouragement, feedback and generous support you need to reach your full potential. Here are the 5 types of individuals that should comprise what I call your G.R.A.N.D. circle of relationships.

- **Godfather** – This is someone who believes in you and acts as your sponsor and advocate at the senior levels of your organization when key decisions that affect you are being made.

- **Really Good Headhunters** – These individuals comprise your plan B in case you want to explore the HR marketplace or you need to find your next HR job in a hurry.
- **Advisors and Mentors** – These are simply people you've built a relationship with who've been in your shoes before who can provide advice, support and the savvy gained from experience.
- **Your Network** –These are individuals that are already part of your circle of relationships. However, your goal should be to maintain contact with these people and expand the number of them over time.
- **Direct Boss** – The person you report to right now. This individual will have more impact than anyone else over whether you succeed or fail in your current role.

We will describe each of these people in detail in Chapters 17-21 and how to best utilize them to maximize your HR success.

Unwritten HR Rule #16

Lone rangers don't travel far up the HR ladder of success. You need to have a support system consisting of a G.R.A.N.D. network of relationships. These include:

- *A Godfather*
- *Really Good Headhunters*
- *Advisors and Mentors*
- *Your Network*
- *Direct Boss*

17

HR CAREER GODFATHERS: WHAT THEY DO & HOW THEY WORK

Godfathers -- or the "G" in your G.R.A.N.D. network -- are commonly referred to as sponsors in most organizations. I call them godfathers because, to me, that more clearly describes the role they play in your HR career

A godfather believes in you and acts as your advocate at senior levels of the organization when key decisions that affect you are being made. They carry a lot of weight, are in the room or at the table when your name comes up in discussions about succession, promotions.... and yes, even decisions about who gets whacked (much like what Marlon Brando did as the real *Godfather* in the movie). They are inner-circle players and, depending on your level, are typically vice presidents or higher.

Before you accuse me of being sexist, women are of course godfathers too.

As godfathers sit in these critical meetings that decide your career, they help make the tough calls and are in a position to speak objectively and favorably about you. They can also defend you from critics in the room who may not be in your corner.

Let me give you an example.

Years ago, we were chartered by our CEO to reduce HR headcount by 10%, just like every other department in our company. I gathered with my fellow HR leadership team executives in our large board room. We spent two days (and evenings) discussing every single one of the 160 HR professionals in our organization. As each HR person's name was called, unless an HR executive spoke out on that person's behalf, vouching for his or her performance, potential and value to the company, that person was canned. Clearly, poor performers or those in less essential HR roles were let go. *And so were those without godfathers to speak up on their behalf.*

One HR senior executive told me afterwards, "You know something, that was a bloodbath. Someone's career can get destroyed in 19 seconds in one of these meetings." I agreed. And he went on to further say...

"If You Don't Have Someone In That Room That Jumps To Your Defense, Puts Any Setbacks You've Had In Perspective Or Champions Strongly For You, Your Career Is Cooked!"

He was right. And, that's what godfathers do.

The same thing happens when it comes to promotions. People without godfathers generally don't get to the next level.

Let me further illustrate the power of having a godfather as it relates to getting promoted.

As I was writing this book, in return for anonymity, Jim R., agreed to share his experience as a godfather. Jim is a long-time friend of mine and senior vice president of HR at one of America's most recognized companies (not Pepsi). He also gave me access to Julie, one of his direct reports, so that I could get her perspective also.

Here's their story.

While working in Jim's organization, Julie's passion for results and people skills immediately grabbed his attention. Clients who worked with her raved about how great she was to work with and how proactive she was on issues. At the time, she was an HR manager in a generalist role, accountable for the company's Chicago plant with 400 employees. Julie, who today is the company's vice president of talent management, at that time was just another member of Jim's team. She had no idea how truly impressed he was by her performance and potential – until after her first year in her plant HR job.

"Because of the job I had, I was one of 20 HR managers reporting up through Jim's organization. He was always very busy, so while we had some natural direct interaction, there wasn't one single moment when he sat me down and said, 'Hey, I'm going to be your godfather,'" Julie told me when I talked with her.

"I just began noticing that he was very supportive of me, calling me sometimes out of the blue to ask my advice on some big labor situation at another plant or assigning me to HR projects at headquarters – all while expecting me to continue to do my HR job at the plant. Based on his feedback, I also knew he often spoke very positively about me in succession planning discussions with the senior HR leadership team."

What Jim told me was that he was very impressed with Julie's track record and potential even before she even joined his organization. In fact, when the company was recruiting to fill the Chicago plant HR position, Jim told Julie's direct boss to keep the job open for two months until Julie was ready to come onboard. In doing this, Jim took a lot of heat from the executive vice president of manufacturing who felt he needed to fill that plant's HR leader role right away.

Jim stood firm and pushed back.

"I couldn't afford to simply put a warm body in that job. We were looking to improve the diversity at the senior levels of HR and we had plenty of internal candidates who could do the Chicago job. But that wasn't what we needed. That was too short sighted. We needed someone exceptional who could not only do the Chicago job, but someone with the potential move two to three levels above this position into a much more senior HR role. I was convinced Julie was that person," Jim told me.

"I thought she was a high potential right from the start, bright, poised, terrific with people, innovative, great track record of results and unafraid to tackle tough issues. All she needed was someone to guide, champion, and help open doors for her with the senior folks in the organization. "

In essence, she needed a godfather.

So, Jim stepped in and without telling Julie until years later, he became her godfather, sponsor and advocate. Behind the scenes, he helped steer her career and worked with her boss to ensure she got the right assignments. He also used his considerable senior influence to put her on the "right" company-wide projects with visibility to the top brass so that they could see her in action too.

All of this wouldn't have happened unless Julie delivered on her end. And she did, in spades. After spending 18 months in the plant HR leader's job, Julie was then promoted to director of HR with accountability for 9 sites and 2100 employees. This was clearly a stretch assignment but with Jim's influence and mentors he asked to guide her, she started slow but later excelled. And, three years after this assignment she was promoted to her current role as VP of talent management. In this position, she works directly with Jim and the senior team on the leadership development strategy for the entire company. With the new title and role, this 36-year-old, married mother of two is the youngest person ever promoted into that job and the first Hispanic female in the company's history at that level.

She credits her own willingness to stretch herself and Jim's persistent influence as key factors in helping to elevate her career so quickly.

"I wasn't consciously looking for someone to be my godfather. I didn't even know what one was. But having one has clearly been an enabler for me and has been beneficial to my career progression," offers Julie. "I was able to have doors open for me and opportunities made available to me that I don't think would have happened."

Julie is now a godfather for two junior HR people within the company. One is a senior HR manager, the other a labor attorney. As Jim did with her, she has chosen not to tell them about this, but instead is operating with them quietly behind the scenes. On occasion, she'll have lunch or dinner with each of them. She might call them up to check in on how they're doing or to get help on a project she's working on. They know she is sincerely interested in their careers. Most importantly, she keeps tabs on their performance through their managers to ensure that they are worthy of her help.

Secrets You Should Know
About The Role of Godfathers
In Your HR Career

Godfathers are important for anyone in HR, but critical for women of color. The fact that Julie is a Hispanic woman is important. Women of color, in particular, are finding that having godfathers or sponsors mean the difference between getting ahead and hitting their head on a cement ceiling. While these barriers are coming down every day, there is still much more progress needed.

"Women, especially women of color, don't advance in organizations without sponsorship. Even in staff roles like HR. It just doesn't happen," says Vanessa Weaver-Coleman Ph.D., CEO of Alignment Strategies, a Washington, D.C.-based management consulting firm. "So when you want to move into executive level positions, you've got to have a sponsor--and not just one because the decision about who advances is often made by more than one person. So if you have more than one sponsor, it really increases the chances that you will get the nod."

After talking with Julie, I really believe that she still would have ultimately made it to the HR executive suite...just not as quickly. She clearly is a talented HR executive. However, the plum assignments and the visibility to her company's senior team that she received so early in her career would not have happened without Jim's help. So Jim's role as a godfather in her career was crucial.

There's a big difference between mentors and godfathers. Mentors are people you choose. Godfathers are executives who choose you. Both are people who believe in you, have your best interests at heart and look out after you. But there's a difference. When you have godfathers higher up the HR hierarchy, you are nearly bulletproof. Not only can they bail your butt out of trouble, they'll keep you from getting into trouble in the first place by offering good advice. It's like having a life raft in place when the waters get choppy and a riverboat guide who will help you navigate the rising and falling tides of the organization.

Since you cannot go out and recruit a godfather, you must attract one to you. And, as you might suspect, this is a long term process that won't happen overnight. But with that said, here are some helpful hints:

- **Having a godfather always starts with your boss.** When you boss has your back, you get the benefit of the doubt from people up and down the HR org chart. Having your boss in your corner is a great foundation for your reputation and career. However, to be a real trump card for you, your boss should have clear, unmistakable pull with the senior leaders of your organization.

- **If you have senior-level HR mentors already, look for opportunities to potentially convert them into godfathers.** Start by being likeable, helpful and useful. Look for ways to do favors for your mentors. Join project teams or pet projects that they are involved with. This could be anything from helping them fundraise as part of a United Way campaign they're leading to serving on a compensation redesign project they're heading up.

- **Support new senior HR leaders when they first join the organization.** When a new senior HR executive first comes aboard he or she is very vulnerable. They don't know a lot about their new organization. They are trying to build relationships, learn a new culture, take charge, while trying to figure out how to best make their mark. Most will welcome lots of assistance. You can position yourself as a helpful supporter and score some early points by taking the initiative to introduce yourself, buying them coffee, and offering to help them get familiar with your part of the organization.

Become someone worth godfathering. This all starts with performing well in your current role. No one wants to be a godfather to a "B" or "C" player. So, be open to candid feedback. Be willing to take risks. Often, there will be occasions when the godfather's guidance seems risky, so be willing to operate out of the box.

Again, you may or may not ever know that someone has taken you under their wing as your godfather. So always be prepared to support, acknowledge, and respond quickly to requests from senior members of the organization. First of all, if you don't do this you're committing career suicide. And, secondly, this request may be coming from your self-appointed godfather, who is just lurking in the shadows.

Unwritten HR Rule #17

Having a godfather is crucial to your HR career. Godfathers are people who believe in you, act as your advocate and sponsor you at the senior levels of the organization when key career decisions about you are being made. Unlike mentors, you cannot choose a godfather, they choose you.

18

TWO PEOPLE YOU MUST ALWAYS KEEP ON SPEED DIAL

Question: As an HR professional, who should you always have on speed dial? Answer: Two good headhunters.

Really good headhunters are the "R" in your G.R.A.N.D. network. (Okay, I admit I fudged on this part of the acronym a little bit).

Even if you already have a great HR job, if you don't have a plan for getting your next HR gig all lined up, right here, right now, at this very moment, then you're an idiot.

Someone Once Told Me That In Today's Economy, A Full-Time HR Job Is Merely A Temporary One Disguised With Benefits

Let's be candid. The only things you can count on now for certain are death, taxes, and reductions in force. In today's tough, "short-term-live-and-die-by-stock-price-culture," things change in an instant. You are just one re-org away from being on the street. You are only one job elimination away from being handed your pink slip. And, you can be fairly sure that your current HR job is probably not your last.

If you go to work tomorrow morning unprepared to leave that afternoon, then you have your head in the sand. It's a mistake not to be mindful of the possibility that today could be your final day at your company.

For this reason, executive recruiters or headhunters (or whatever you choose to call them) should be an important part of your network – and working with them is a skill you need to master. They are important part of your Plan B, should you find yourself suddenly in the job market.

You're In HR, So You Probably Know This Already... But Just In Case You Need A Refresher, Here Is A Quick Primer On Recruiting Firms and Headhunters

Retained firms generally focus on senior executive searches and are paid by their client company, whether the search is successful or not. A portion of the fee is normally paid upfront, with the balance due over a predetermined time.

Contingency firms are paid only if a client company hires one of their candidates.

Generally both firms are paid on a percentage of the first year's income. In other words, a $100,000 per year salary will fetch the recruiter $30,000 at a 30% fee rate. Fees can range anywhere from 5% to 33% or more.

Retained firms usually concentrate on positions paying in excess of $150,000 and contingency firms on less than $150,000.

The major difference you need to be aware of is this: contingency firms may decide to proactively market you to their clients or to a specific geographic market. They will assume all the costs and all the risk in doing so, while retained firms generally will not do this.

What does this mean to you?

Simply put, it means if you decide you want to have a recruiter market you, you had better be outstanding in your area of expertise and cooperative.

Strategies For Building Relationships
And Working With Headhunters

Dig the well before you're thirsty. Like most relationships, you will want to create a relationship with headhunters well before you need them. You're probably wasting everyone's time talking to a headhunter unless you're at least thinking about making a job change, but the absolute worst time to make first contact is when you need a new job right away! The purpose of a first contact is to let the headhunter know that you exist, give them some idea of your talents and let them know you're exploring opportunities but you're in no big hurry. The best way to use a headhunter is *strategically* when you have a six month runway in front of you.

Have your two headhunters on speed dial. They can be your "ears" as to hiring trends in the industry. Relationships with recruiters go both ways. If you help them recruit by providing referrals, they can also recruit for you someday -- whether it's helping to staff your team, or finding the next job for you. Either way, it's another win-win situation. Because of their level and frequency of contact with other job seekers and hiring companies, you get "linked" indirectly to their network of company contacts. And that's obviously a good thing.

Don't ignore them. If you're not looking for a new HR job, it's easy to blow off their phone calls. Don't fall in this trap. The quickest way to drive headhunters away from you is by ignoring them. They are used to having their calls unreturned, and so, by calling them back you stay top of mind. So, if they call you, return their call as soon as you can. If they email you, respond back quickly. If you're out of the office, activate your auto response which will let them know that. If you're not interested in the job, acknowledge this quickly so they can move on. And by all means, if you're not interested, and you know a person that is a better fit, provide them with this name as a referral.

Always act professionally. Perhaps the biggest mistake HR people make when working with recruiters is not trying very hard to impress them. A headhunter isn't finding you a job because they like your humorous personality, this is their living. And they only get paid to supply quality candidates to a client company. And they are not going to risk putting you in front of their top-dollar clients if they're not sure you can present yourself professionally. So act like you're on a job interview when you meet with a headhunter because you *are*. Be professional and leave the sandals, shorts or baseball cap at home.

Always have an updated resume posted online ready to go. We've talked about this already, but it can't be reiterated enough. LinkedIn is a great tool for doing this. Your LinkedIn profile is a marketing tool so make sure it stays updated. Most savvy headhunters are doing keyword searches on LinkedIn before cold calling candidates or spending a dime on anything else. So you want to easily make yourself found. Some HR people allow their profile to get out of date when they're not looking for a job and that hurts them. If you're not looking for work, you can let the recruiters know that after they've contacted you. Posting an updated resume online lets you continue to expand your network to prepare for your next job change.

Sell your results. To help headhunters work best on your behalf, you need to show how great you are so that they can target a job that's a great match. So, sell yourself and what you've accomplished. Simply put, be prepared to provide your recruiter with the answers to two questions: "What HR initiatives have you led?" and "How have you helped generate revenues or save costs?" You'll move into a new HR role quickly if you can show quantifiable, hard-cold results.

Present yourself as the best candidate for the job – period. Job hunters often make the mistake of thinking that a recruiter is their best buddy. He or she is not. Act the same way you would in a regular job interview: Don't express anger about your current job situation, don't trash your current employer, and don't blame other people for your mistakes. A headhunter isn't your therapist or your spouse. Good recruiters represent the best interests of the clients who've hired them to fill a position. So to get them to work hard for you, come across as the top quality candidate that they'd be proud to present to their clients.

Do your homework. You'll waste your time and the headhunter's time if you are unprepared to discuss your work history and provide documentation of previous employment. Don't be vague about how many years you spent at the company you left to join your current firm. Make sure you have contact information for at least three professional references.

If your headhunter has produced an interview for you, probe – hard! You'll probably have a zillion questions about how the whole process works, and that's actually a good thing. Every headhunter has a slightly different way of handling the interview process. So, as any other interviewer would, a recruiter will welcome your questions because it demonstrates that you're interested. Make sure you receive as much information as possible from your recruiter before you go in front of a potential employer. Your recruiter likely not only knows pertinent details about the organization -- what their products and services are -- but also something about the hiring manager, the business and the HR team who will be interviewing you. Ask, too, if other people have interviewed for this job and what mistakes they may have made.

Provide the headhunter with your compensation expectations. Most people find it hard to discuss salary and that's fine. I've found that HR folks, in particular, like to keep this information under wraps. However, a headhunter once told me that there at least three people in this world that need to know your current salary: the IRS, your spouse and your headhunter, (actually, I'm not convinced the first two need to know, but I'm sure I'm in the minority). Headhunters need this information because they need to exclude you from all jobs under your salary level. If you play cat-and-mouse with them, you'll get branded as a diva – and you'll get absolutely nowhere. Great headhunters know how to deal with your salary appropriately to get you what you're worth. Years ago, I knew a terrific senior HR manager who was making $85,000. She was grossly underpaid and under-appreciated. She went on an interview set up by a headhunter she had a great relationship with and got an offer for $135,000. She was floored, and couldn't believe that was what she was worth. (By the way, this clearly doesn't happen every day). I understand the salary midpoint for the job was $150,000, so they didn't overpay for her skills. More importantly, if they had known what she was making at the time, they wouldn't have made an offer because they would have concluded she was too "light" for the position. Incidentally, she's done a fabulous job and has since been promoted to HR Director.

Don't waste your headhunter's time. Use your headhunter just for recruiting. If you need career counseling, talk to one of your mentors, advisors, or a career counselor. Good headhunters don't have the time. They are constantly inundated with requests for free career counseling, free resume writing advice, free practice interview sessions, free job leads, and the like. While most of them are more than qualified in all these areas, their "real" job is to hunt heads for their client companies. Don't think you're doing them a favor by letting them "have a look at your resume early" or "getting the opportunity to market you". That's not how they feed their families. If you know their game ahead of time, your odds of winning with them are greatly increased.

Unwritten HR Rule #18

You should always have two good headhunters on speed dial. They are an important part of your Plan B strategy, should you find yourself suddenly thrusted into the job market.

19

UTILIZING ADVISORS & MENTORS TO TAKE YOUR HR CAREER TO THE NEXT LEVEL

I've never met a successful HR leader who has not had at least two profoundly influential advisors or mentors in their lives. HR professionals that have mentors have an edge over those that don't. They perform better on the job. They get promoted more quickly. They earn higher salaries. And they report more job and career satisfaction.

Advisors and mentors are the "A" in your G.R.A.N.D. network.

Dr. Dave Thomas, a Harvard business professor and consultant to our HR team at Pepsi, concurs. He has done extensive research on corporate mentoring. He found that managers, especially minority managers, whose careers advanced the farthest generally were beneficiaries of the best networks of mentors and advisors.

So, the question shouldn't be whether you should have them. The question should be how many of them should you have. And my answer is: as many as possible! (Please note: while some people differentiate between an advisor and a mentor, they are so similar I use the terms interchangeably. But for ease of understanding, I'll use mentor for the rest of this chapter.)

Mentors are simply people who've been in your shoes before and can offer advice, support and the savvy gained from experience. So acquiring them should be one of your highest career development priorities.

Each of your mentors should know you and be familiar with your job and company. It's important that you trust and respect them, because over time you are going to reveal to them a lot about yourself and your ambitions.

Mentors can be found in any walk of life. You might have a peer or buddy who is especially on the ball. You might have an awesome boss. Your dad might have a friend who just seems to know everyone. A customer or vendor could take an interest in your career. Years ago, Jack Welch, when he was GE's chairman, became an expert on how digitization could contribute to his company's success by getting mentored by an internet computer geek who was just 25 years old – half of Jack's age at the time. So, don't get hung up on age or labels.

Your best bet for a mentor is a regular, reachable person you know who buys into your potential and is willing to spend time with you, sharing knowledge, encouraging you, helping you make connections and providing inspiration.

Let me tell you about someone I worked with that met all of these criteria.

How Pam Hewitt's Advice, Mentoring & Candid Feedback Helped Me Advance My Career

Pam Hewitt was the senior vice-president of human resources at Quaker for three years. Today, as a retired HR executive she occasionally consults with large companies across the U.S. on senior human resources issues. She's been a colleague, my boss and a great friend. However, I want to talk about one critical role she has played as a mentor.

First, some background. Shortly after Bob Morrison, the new Quaker CEO arrived from Kraft Foods, he reorganized the company and named a new senior vice president of HR. It was Pam. Pam had joined Quaker a few years before this after having had prior HR leadership roles with the Urban League, Container Corporation, Nabisco/Nestle, and KFC. Bob was impressed with her breadth of HR experience and her ability to provide the HR leadership for the changes he envisioned. Ironically, I knew Pam's husband Warren, when he and I worked at Inland Steel years earlier.

In any event, I was delighted to see a colleague of mine move into the top HR job. And I was even more excited when I learned she would be reorganizing the HR function and putting in place her new HR leadership team.

As an HR director at the time, I thought this was a great opportunity for me to move into the VP HR job supporting the supply chain and manufacturing organization. This would be a significant promotion for me. Next to Pam's job, this was the second biggest HR job in the company. And I thought I had a great shot at it.

However, a few days before she was to announce her new team, Pam called me into her office and showed me her new org chart. I was not in the VP role. Instead, I was shown continuing in my current job reporting now, not to Pam, but to a "TBD." This meant she'd be putting someone else, not yet named, into the job I coveted.

Very disappointed at this turn of events, Pam shared her rationale. She told me very supportively and yet very directly: "Alan, I admire what you've done as a generalist HR director for Quaker Foods. You are very skilled in OD. And, you've made some great contributions to the organization, but you don't have the depth of labor relations experience that this job requires. With our heavy union labor negotiations agenda, I can't risk putting you in this job."

As much as I hated getting this feedback, I really couldn't really argue with it. Labor was the one area on my resume that was shallow. She was right.

But the discussion wasn't over.

She continued by saying: "I'm going to continue my outside search to fill this VP HR job. It's a critical for the organization. But, at the same time, I'd like to help you build your labor relations skills so that you can be a candidate for this role down the road. And while I can't make any guarantees, I have confidence in you and I'll do everything I can to help you get ready for the VP job."

With her guidance, over the next few weeks and months, we laid out an aggressive, personal development program geared to deepen my experience in labor relations. Fortunately, I had some tough labor contracts of my own coming up in the Foods division. And, so just doing this part of my job well would provide a great opportunity to show her more of what I could do.

But we didn't stop at using my job to develop me. With Pam's help, we planned specific labor relations workshops I should attend; contracted with a couple of Pam's former mentors to provide one-on-one coaching; and scheduled time on our calendars for me to receive on-going feedback and counsel directly from Pam herself.

Seventeen months from the date of our original discussion about the job, Pam still hadn't found the candidate she was looking for. During that time, I continued developing my labor skills and led the delivery of three very successful labor contracts at our Cedar Rapids, St. Joseph and Danville locations. But even so, I was still shocked when during one of our coaching sessions, she told me that because of my great progress, she believed I was now ready and would like to promote me into the VP job.

Wow! To say I was surprised would be a gross understatement.

But there was one last hurdle.

She indicated that I'd need to meet with Bob Morrison, the new CEO, who had the power to veto all new VP appointments. Pam had already recommended me. But rather than leave this to chance, she helped me "prepare" for my lunch meeting with Bob.

With her assistance, I passed the lunch "interview" and was named her new vice president of HR for Supply Chain organization...the job I admit I wasn't ready for seventeen months before.

As I think back over this experience, though Pam was my boss, her role as an advisor and mentor me in this situation was significant. She exhibited all the qualities you would look for in a mentor.

- She had experience, credibility and influence in the organization.
- She was willing to be brutally candid, direct and specific in her feedback.
- She was equally willing to provide encouragement, direction and inspiration.
- She spent time following up to check my progress and provided coaching and advice.
- She shared her own personal network of advisors and contacts.
- She helped me craft a plan that could lead to success.
- She imparted her knowledge and readily shared her own experiences.
- She directed me to specific training that could help me.
- She was a sounding board when I encountered roadblocks.

"Typically mentors have a wider viewpoint than the person they are mentoring, so they can see opportunities before you might get wind of them," says Donna Fowler, national president of the Professional Coaches and Mentors Association. "They have influence with people who you may need in order to get those opportunities or those projects. And they can work through the organization and teach you how to do it," she says.

Clearly, Pam played an important role in advancing my career in HR and today she is one of my most cherished friends.

Here Are Additional Unwritten HR Rules In Utilizing Advisors and Mentors To Advance Your HR Career

Get extraordinarily clear on your career direction. Before you can be mentored, you must know what HR success for you looks like, so you can recognize it when you get there. For example: Do you want to ultimately head up the HR function for your company? Your division? Or your department? Do you see yourself on an HR generalist or on a specialist career path? What personal sacrifices (relocation, family time, additional education, extra hours on evenings and weekends) are you willing to make for your career? Be specific. Nail this down. Realize that few busy people want to waste time or put in the effort to help you figure out what you want to be when you grow up. Most don't mind sharing with you advice on how to get there, but determining where you want to go is your responsibility.

Pinpoint the right people who can help you get there. When selecting people who can help you achieve your goals, pick mentors who by nature are either givers or at the least reciprocators. You can recognize them by how they behave – do they give others credit, are they glass half-full people, do they energize those around them (or do they sap energy). If so, these are the people you want to target as mentors. Some of the best mentors are often people you work with whom you just gravitate towards naturally. They're likeable, bright and generous with their time. You admire what they've accomplished and feel comfortable around them. They may not be in your immediate work group or even in your department. But you like the way they operate and feel as if you could learn from them.

Avoid advisors or mentors who are just not that into you. Vernon Jordan, one of the premier Civil Rights activists of our time and a former head of the Urban League, readily admits that when Barack Obama asked for his presidential endorsement, he said no and advised him not to run. When asked why, he responded that he didn't feel that it was "Barack's time." Think about where Obama's career would be today had he heeded this advice. So be wary of the expert who can only tell you why you will fail and why you can't do what you want to do. Such people have to be "big" enough not to be jealous or envious of your success and accomplishments. They have to be smart enough to know what they do not know, and secure enough to admit it.

You must drive the mentoring relationship, not your mentor. Come prepared when working with a mentor. Mentors are busy people who have careers and obligations of their own. Also, they can't help you in every area of your life. Every time you meet with your mentor, you should have an agenda that you've written out so that you can focus your discussion in those areas. Also be prepared to give your mentor an update on how you've executed against suggestions they offered at your last meeting.

Aim to create a diverse board of mentors. It's unlikely that one single person will be able to meet all your professional development needs. So, you should plan to have more than one mentor and different mentors as you progress and develop your HR career. Your mentors can and should be very diverse in their backgrounds, experiences, genders, and ages. But one thing should be consistent. They should all have the ability to inspire, challenge, stretch, and move you into action. Do you have people like this in your life? If not, you're at a severe disadvantage compared to your HR peers who do have these types of guiding voices they can draw upon.

Don't get hung up on making mentoring so formal. Let me tell you something you might find strange. Personally, in my entire HR career spanning 25 years, I never, ever asked anyone to be my mentor. Now don't get me wrong. I am thankful to have had countless mentors in my career. And I wouldn't have been able to move my career forward without their valuable career advice, counsel and friendship. But asking someone to mentor me always felt awkward and uncomfortable. So early in my career a retiring senior HR executive gave me some advice about mentors that I've never forgotten. Here it is: "Get to know the decisions makers in the company, before you need their help. Set up time to talk to them about the business, about your interests, and about their needs. *But, don't call this rela-*

tionship anything. Don't label it. It's not mentoring. It's not networking. It's not ass-kissing. It's just two people getting to know each other. Don't make it formal. Simply set these people up by asking: 'Would you mind if I stop by from time to get your advice about the business, projects you're working on and my career.' That's it. Keep it simple." I've followed this advice almost to the letter. And, no one has ever told me "no." And I never abused the access they gave me.

Once you have a mentor relationship going, take good care of it. Set up regular dates for coffee with your mentor. Keep him or her apprised of your progress, challenges, and questions. Use them as sounding boards. Share your frustrations (constructively) and ask for advice on how to deal with them. But be sure every discussion you have isn't about some huge issue or major crisis. Your mentor is there to help nurture you in your job and career, not to help bail you out every time you have to put out a fire.

Make mentoring a two-way street by helping your mentor succeed. Many productive mentoring relationships have benefits for both people. This is where some mentees mess up. Instead of looking for what you can get, think about what you can *give.* Figure out what you can do for your mentor that will help them in their own career, personal lives, or with the legacy they may want to leave with the organization. Volunteering to join task forces that they lead is one example. Or offering to take on assignments or projects they don't have time to do is another. You might also pass on articles that they might be interested in based on conversations you may have had. Sharing perspectives that they may not get from other places can also help. Anything that you can do to proactively put their needs before your own makes for an excellent and long-term mentor-mentee relationship.

Seek mentors from different disciplines – within and outside of HR. HR leaders who have overcome career obstacles can be valuable mentors, but so can those with different speciali-zations in HR. If you're a compensation manager, it may be helpful to get a mentor from OD. Get someone whose expertise is different than yours. Also, seek out mentors from line man-agement. You might look for a mentor in finance, marketing, IT or sales, someone who has done really well in their field. Many successful HR professionals have benefitted from mentors with general business experience. The HR mentor can provide useful insights about other areas within HR, while the business mentors can provide guidance from the perspective of the overall busi-ness.

Take advantage of your organization's formal mentoring programs. Some companies have a formal mentoring program where executive and managers are assigned to high potential employees. This is similar to the faculty-student arrangement you may have had in college, which is an obligation on the part of both parties rather than an option. Sometimes these work. Sometimes they don't. In any event, if you have an opportunity to participate, seize it.

Finally, when mentors drop off, think of them as "gra-duating" not as a loss. As time passes, some of your advisors and mentors may fall off your radar or become less engaged. It's perfectly normal. Don't take it personally. People's busi-ness priorities and career interests change. So, when a mentor drops out of your life, just cherish the time you spent learning from each other as a great mutual education period. And, make sure you learned something from the experience that added value to your career. You should get back in the game and reach out to someone new as a replacement. And, keep in mind that just because someone falls away for a while doesn't means he or she might not come back to play a major role in your HR career at some point in the future.

Unwritten HR Rule #19

Don't hesitate to fully utilize advisors and mentors to take your HR career to the next level. Attract the ones you want by keeping the relationship informal, taking good care of the relationship and by looking for ways to help them succeed.

"Avoid mentors who belittle your HR ambitions. Poor mentors do that. The great ones make you feel, that you too, can become great!"

20

NETWORKING STRATEGIES JUST FOR HR PROFESSIONALS

In building your G.R.A.N.D. circle of relationships, the "N" stands for your Network. In this chapter, you'll find some terrific tips and strategies for nurturing and growing the number of people in your network that can help advance your HR career.

A confession: I was going to write this chapter myself until I came across Sandy Jones-Kaminski. After reading her white paper: "12 Rules of Networking for HR Professionals," I concluded that no one else could do justice to this topic (including me) and that it absolutely had to be included in this book.

So with her permission, in this chapter you can now benefit from the nuggets of wisdom in her white paper.

But first, here's what you should know about Sandy. She is a self-described networking enthusiast and is the principal consultant of Bella Domain, LLC, a recent VP of Networking for one of the largest chapters of the American Marketing Association. She's also a HR industry vet with experience as an executive level outsourced HR services provider and as an executive manager of in-house HR. And more importantly for you, Sandy is an expert at networking.

She adds: "For some, this will be a refresher, but for all, this chapter will offer some valuable insights on what to do, and just as importantly, what not to do while you're out there working hard to build good social capital and grow and nurture your valuable network as an HR professional. You'll also learn why you might want to become a 'pay it forward' focused person, as well as how to be more memorable while putting forth all that effort." So now without further ado, here are...

12 Rules of Networking for HR Professionals
By Sandy Jones-Kaminski
of Bella Domain, LLC

Did you know you are an ambassador?

As a professional in the HR arena you undoubtedly recognize that a large part of your role is to be an ambassador for your company as well as for your own personal brand, both inside and outside of the office.

It's important for you to think about how you want people to perceive you within your company, the community in which you live, and even online. Are you known for being helpful, responsive, fun, smart, compliance-savvy, resourceful, emotionally intelligent, persuasive, empathic or maybe even well-connected?

A smart HR pro gets clear on the reputation and values they want to cultivate and then works hard to demonstrate them each and every day. How can you practice communicating your personal brand to the world? Well, one sure-fire way we know is via networking.

Why Networking?

While networking may have once been the domain of sales and marketing, and was for a long time considered solely a marketing and business development function, today, networking matters to just about everyone. Does networking mean you're looking to use people to achieve selfish goals, or opportunistically ask people for help? No, of course not. And, to be clear, let's start with the definition of the word network according to The Oxford Dictionary: *nétwerk* n. & v. a group of people who exchange information, contacts, and experience for professional or social purposes.

Therefore, networking can be defined as one's efforts to create this group, and of course it can be done honestly and considerately. In fact, almost all your networking can help other people as much as it can help you. In any industry or career level, networking helps you make connections in a personal way. It aids you in building relationships of support and respect and enables you to discover and create mutually beneficial connections. Early in their careers, folks in both of the disciplines mentioned earlier, learn that you never know where you might meet that next key contact, partner, client or even friend. It's a mindset no serious HR professional can be without.

Another way to think about networking is as the deliberate process of making connections for mutual benefit. However, whether you network to make friends (new to town), find a new job, source candidates, develop your current career, explore new career options, obtain referrals, or simply to broaden your professional horizons, it is important to focus on networking as an exchange of information, contacts or experiences. Remember, instead of thinking "What can I get out of this?" also think, "What can I give to this?" whenever possible.

In the case of HR pros, many of the people attending live events or participating in an online discussion could be potential employees, clients, vendors, or sources of referral for any of these things. And, while today, networking occurs as much online as it does off line, we're not going to differentiate in this chapter. Just use your good judgment to apply these 12 rules wherever they might be applicable, and as a general rule, it's always best that you don't do or say anything online that you wouldn't in person.

Networking for HR Pros Rule #1:
Be Memorable

How you introduce yourself will make an impact on the people you meet and will likely help determine whether or not they ac-

tually remember you and/or your company. Practice your introduction whenever you can. (Yes, you need to!) A favorite of a
Director of HR I know goes something like this:

"Hi! I'm Megan James and I'm the official corporate back
watcher at Acme Enterprises." People often then try to guess
what she does (if she's not at a SHRM event), and they usually
think she's corporate counsel or, these days, someone in the ac-
counting realm. A little humor goes a long way in the HR field,
as most of you know, so a tongue-in-cheek opener like this will
not only make you memorable, it will also help create conversation, which often makes things more relaxed.

And, yes, it's always best to strive to develop a casual conversation first. A networking function is an ideal way to get
people to know you. In business, as well as in personal dealings,
it is in everyone's best interest to make an effort to try to create a
relaxed and personal environment in which to introduce yourself
or your company. Referencing cocktail party or wedding guest
small talk will help you come up with a few easy conversation
starters. Try openers like, "So, Bob, how are you connected to
the host(s)?" or, "What brought you to this particular event out
of the many going on in town?"

Believe it or not, another smart way to be memorable, as well
as productive, is to wear something to the event in a bright color
or that is unique, such as a shirt with a print or pattern. Most
folks will have an easier time pointing you out to others during
the event and then also remembering you when you follow-up
with them after. My follow-up emails often include, "Hi Barry,
I was the gal wearing the red scarf and jacket in that group of
four we were part of Tuesday morning."

And, probably most importantly, get comfortable with small
talk if you aren't already. Most people in the HR industry already are pretty adept at putting others at ease, and if they're not,
they sure should be. After all, in most cases you're often the
first person a new employee comes in contact with both before
and after they are hired. I say practice everywhere you can. This
includes places like the grocery store, on an airplane, or at a
lunch counter. Think about setting a goal to speak to at least one

stranger every day. You can choose to initiate, but even something as simple as "I'm fine, thanks, and how about you?" counts as a conversation starting response.

Networking for HR Pros Rule #2:
Always Have A Goal

You can also strive to make in-person networking less stressful, and more enjoyable and beneficial by setting goals around meeting specific people, qualifying prospective employees, collecting certain information, and developing current or new business relationships as well as mutually supportive friendships. Having a mission or goal will help create focus, which usually helps relieve nervousness. Whatever you do, keep your expectations reasonable and don't let your valuable time and energy at in-person networking events be wasted.

Let's say you have only one open hiring requisition at this time, and it's for something fairly simple to fill, like a staff accountant, but you know that come the third quarter of this year you'll likely be ramping up again. As you mentally prepare for the event, be sure to set a goal for yourself that you'll share the longer-term plans for future growth with at least two people. You can then encourage the folks you meet to sign up for updates on your company's site or to join your talent pool if you have one online somewhere.

Also, remember, one of the advantages of in-person networking events is that once you tell one person you meet what you're looking for, if you've made a good impression, they'll likely suggest other people find you as they work their way around the event. (Here's where that polka-dot blouse comes in.) Folks often do this when they hear someone new to them speak of something related to you or your recently shared goal.

Networking for HR Pros Rule #3: Offer Help to Others First

While you're clear on your goal, a lot of other folks coming to events have done the same prep work, so think about being the first to ask others what brought them to the event or what it is they need help with these days. For example, you might say: "So, Bob, do you need help with anything in your world right now?" Or perhaps while you are listening to Bob's intro or elevator pitch, a person you know pops into your mind that you realize could be a good resource for him to connect with regarding the best associations to join for recruiting electrical engineers (your brother-in-law maybe). Well, offer to connect Bob to them and simply consider it an easy "pay it forward" in the karma bank. Because, when you're least expecting it, you'll soon likely be the recipient of some good karma of your own.

Networking for HR Pros Rule #4:
Always Be Sure To Follow-up

Often, the real value of the networking event is found as much in the follow-up as in the active participation at the event. Be sure to keep any promises you may have made to the individuals you met. Perhaps you promised to email an article of interest or a vendor resource to someone. You may have invited someone to join you for a one-on-one conversation about your current list of open hiring reqs or just to have an opportunity for collaboration. Or through your listening and questioning you may have determined good vendor partners for your company's needs. Within one week, give them a call, or write and snail mail them a note, or send an email with the relevant info or item to them included, along with a specific, targeted link to your site.

Bonus Tip: Should you decide you want to connect in-person with a new contact, and are the one extending the invitation, be sure to at least offer to pay for their coffee, lunch or first cocktail. In the many conversations I have with people about networking, or what some folks call "brain picking" sessions, this is definitely one of their biggest pet peeves. Oh, and do your homework on them or their business, especially if you need their help. Most people find it a huge waste of time to start an informal connecting meeting only to be asked to "tell me about

Acme Enterprises" when it's all there on a website or within LinkedIn.

Networking for HR Pros Rule #5:
Keep It Consistent

Try to keep your offline professional brand consistent with your online "professional" personal brand. For most folks, we're talking about LinkedIn here. One of the worst things you can do is to create a disconnect between the values and brand you project on LinkedIn and those you project elsewhere. All professionals can benefit from reading Guy Kawasaki's blog post at: blog.guykawasaki.com/2007/01/linkedin_profil.html. This post is about tweaking your profile on LinkedIn. Today, most online profiles need to read just like you do in person.

Networking for HR Pros Rule #6:
Don't Be A Hit and Run

Make an effort to stay in touch or in occasional contact with folks you meet with whom you want to stay connected. Pay attention to things that matter to them. This is the way to create meaningful connections and trusted new contacts.

For example, after you have followed up with a new acquaintance, and are now perhaps connected on LinkedIn, when you notice updates or changes in their status, go ahead and message or email them to comment on their change. It might be congratulations if you notice a new job, name change (perhaps they got married) or maybe a promotion. Or it might be to offer a suggestion about a good job board you spotted in their field, if you know they're looking for a new opportunity or hinted that they would be soon.

Also, be sure to reach out to people when you don't need anything. Networking is about creating, nurturing and building relationships and they need care and feeding.

Networking for HR Pros Rule #7:
Be Present And Mindful...

In the fast-paced world we live in, we've grown accustomed to juggling three or four tasks at once, and often don't give our full attention to the task at hand. While we can often get away with this in our own little worlds, and can fix any mishaps that occur, when we're engaging with other people we need to be fully present. I can't tell you how many eyes I see darting around at events while the person that those eyes belong to is standing either talking or supposedly listening to another person. I recognize that this may be due to ADHD or some illness like it -- but come on people, please don't do that!

My advice is to try using something called "mindfulness" to be fully present. This simply involves being attentive to the moment, listening intently, and slowing down just a tad to be in the present or the "now."

Networking for HR Pros Rule #8:
Online Is Yet Another Great Way, But...

When networking online you really need to pay attention to the impact that tone can have in your digital communications by watching the cheekiness in your messaging, and waiting until you have first established a personal rapport with people. What a shame it would be to turn-off a potentially great new relationship, by losing them over email. Also, be brief! Too many people think the online channel is a replacement for the letters or memos of old. It is not. Today, most people don't even read their messages on a monitor. Instead, they read them hurriedly on a tiny little screen they hold in their hand. Long messages tend to get saved with the intention that they'll be read thoroughly later, but usually end up forgotten because they've become buried in an inbox, or, even worse, saved in a rarely opened folder.

Networking for HR Pros Rule #9:
Don't Waste Your Time

See Rule #2 regarding having a goal or goals so you don't waste your precious time and energy. Don't go to a networking event unprepared. Try to research the types of people that will be there, and the format of the event. Also, focus on making connections of quality, not quantity.

It's also just as important to disconnect from the unproductive or overly opportunistic and one-sided networking relationships you'll unfortunately come across. And, for the latter, often, just by association, you could attract more unwanted attention or perceptions that you don't want. Don't spend any more time on connections you make when you recognize that there's a suspicious or questionable agenda, or they simply aren't reciprocating. Just move on, and whatever you do, don't take it personally. Today's economy has many people coming from a slightly desperate position, and it's best to just forgive their tactics and practice empathy when you can, but you also don't need to let others take advantage of you. Trust your gut and move on.

Like most folks I know, I'd much rather have someone that's not interested in building a meaningful connection with me come right out and tell me they want to meet my brother-in-law (BIL), the head of Engineering at Motorola. It's much better than them stalking my Connections list on LinkedIn, and then trying to reach him by dropping my name during a cold call or email. My BIL, of course, tells me about it, and then I have that persons' eyebrow-raising methods reflected on me ("Nice friends, Sandy." he says). Not to mention that they now likely have my bad mojo out there on them.

Please don't misunderstand, I recommend being an "open networker" in that you are open to helping people get what they are looking for; they just need to tell you what it is first and at least offer a two-way street if they can. I say be happy to connect with people if they manage to build a relationship through the getting-to-know-you process. Just don't let people "leverage" your contacts without your permission.

Networking for HR Pros Rule #10:
Get Involved in Something

If you haven't joined at least one association connected to your company's industry or your potential future industry, you need to. Being a member of SHRM or EMA is great, but think about targeting groups where your interests will be piqued or your expertise will standout and/or be valued. It'll be a completely different experience. Think: Big fish, small pond here.

In the don't-waste-your-time vein, I advise really getting involved with some of the groups or associations you have joined or have been thinking about joining. Boy, talk about some meaningful connections. When you work shoulder-to-shoulder with others in a volunteer capacity, the vibe is totally different. Plus, you'd be surprised how little of a time investment most professional volunteering actually requires. Don't use your fear of not being able to give enough time as an excuse to not get involved. If you do, you'll miss out on developing meaningful connections or trusted relationships with people with whom you want to network. Besides, today so much help or participation happens online or via phone, so it's never been easier to make good impressions or grow your social capital.

Networking for HR Pros Rule #11:
Get Excited About Networking!

Some days you know you have an event to attend, but you're just spent from a long day of who knows what, or maybe you're questioning whether you have the energy to put on your extrovert face at all. Well, if you think about making progress on your own goals and contributing to your community via the stance of offering help to others first, you can embrace the fact that you're doing good things in the universe. That usually perks anyone up. Remember; initiate the interactions, rather than just responding, and when you're asked what you need help with, you can easily move into the "I'm looking for" role in order to enlist help with your own goals.

Networking for HR Pros Rule #12:
Remember The Details

If you're at a live event and nametags are supplied, be sure you put it on the RIGHT side of your chest. The right side is the correct side because it provides an easy sightline and synchs with your handshake, which, yes, should be firm. We've all experienced the too hard or too limp shake, so please don't be one of those people. That's not a good way to be memorable.

Have a SMILE and some type of business or personal card ready to offer people at all times. And, yes, a pen or pencil can come in handy as well.

Bonus Tip: If you make your own business or personal cards using something easy and inexpensive like VistaPrint, be sure your cards are the type on which you can write with a regular pen. Turns out, another big pet peeve out there is not being able to write on the back of too many of the cards currently in circulation. Many people like to make a note about what you're looking for or how you're connected on the back of the card you give them.

In Closing...

I believe that networking can be a fun and easy way to enrich your life, contribute to your community, broaden your horizons, and enhance your career or business. But, I also believe that it can be potentially devastating to your social capital and personal brand if you act rudely, insensitively, or don't do what you say you are going to do. It is crucial to your success that you treat networking as an exchange of ideas, information and experiences. And, remember, in networking, reciprocity is key, so be generous in sharing your talents, knowledge, and ideas, and always be respectful of and demonstrate appreciation to those around you whether they appear to be able to help you out immediately or not.

Once you get even more comfortable with your networking, you'll probably start chatting people up in line at the post office, in coffee shops, elevators, at parties, well, you name it. It's all great practice and you just never know where your next meaningful connection will come from!

Please feel free to check out the Networking page of www.BellaDomain.com to request a copy of a handy (and free) one-page summary of these 12 Rules of Networking for HR Professionals.

About Sandy Jones-Kaminski and Bella Domain, LLC: Recognized as a connector, networking enthusiast and consummate business development professional, Sandy Jones-Kaminski is very skilled at making connections, building relationships and maximizing opportunities. Sandy is the principal consultant of Bella Domain, LLC, and a recent VP of Networking for one of the largest chapters of the American Marketing Association. She's a HR industry vet with experience as an executive level outsourced HR services provider as well as an executive manager of in-house HR. As a result of having built robust personal and professional networks from scratch three different times during the past ten years, Sandy knows how to make meaningful connections, cultivate relationships, create social capital and host some great networking events. She has built networks in San Francisco, Chicago, and most recently Seattle, where partly due to a local phenomenon called the "Seattle Freeze," she was motivated to start hosting a casual networking event called a PIF (as in pay it forward) Party.

You can reach Sandy via her website www.belladomain.com or phone at (206) 856-5023. You can hire her to help you or your teams with everything from developing a networking or business development strategy, to getting value out of social networking tools, to your own personal branding. She can even help you plan and host your own pay it forward style-networking event.

Sandy is also the creator of Bella Domain's Social Capital Assessment, author of and the soon-to-be-published book by Happy About®, *I'm At A Networking Event – Now What???* which includes a bonus chapter entitled, *How to Have Your Own Networking Event.* Pre-orders for the book can be placed at www.happyabout.info/nowwhat.

Extra Bonus Tip! **If you're in the HR job market now**... there is no better job search strategy than setting up a series of networking meals. It can be very productive to have a quick coffee, lunch or dinner with people in your network and using this time to reconnect with them. Twitter, LinkedIn, and Facebook can advance your brand in HR – but nothing replaces meeting face to face. A contact (or a referral) who remembers that enjoyable lunch you both had can be invaluable by passing on your availability to their contacts and potential hiring managers. However, keep in mind, this isn't an interview – you don't need to sell yourself as the next HR EVP. Just come ready to let them know you're looking and would appreciate any referrals, but let them talk primarily about *themselves*, not you! Use the time to show your genuine interest in them and to just catch up in general. Maybe you'll learn of something with which YOU can help THEM. Most of your contacts would be happy to re-connect on your dime for the purpose of picking their brain. So focus on *them* and save selling yourself for an actual interview.

Unwritten HR Rule #20

Network, network, network...never stop nurturing or expanding your personal and professional connections.

21

LEVERAGING THE MOST
INFLUENTIAL PERSON IN
YOUR HR CAREER

The final piece in building your G.R.A.N.D. network is the "D" which stands for your Direct boss.

Your current boss will have more impact than anyone else on your immediate success in HR. Your boss establishes benchmarks for your success, interprets your actions for other key players, and controls the resources you need. So building a productive working relationship with him or her is an absolute no-brainer.

Some people regard building great chemistry with the boss as sucking up. It doesn't matter what you call it, if done well, it's a very practical career strategy and can turn your manager into your best career advocate...and perhaps even your godfather. And that's what you want.

I had one boss at Pepsi that everyone feared. He was a seasoned, highly respected HR senior executive. Very few people tried to get to know him and my colleagues advised me to do the same. Along with an "untouchable" mystique, he had a reputation of being brutal to work for and tough to satisfy. He had spent a few years as a manufacturing executive, knew the business cold, and didn't take crap from anyone. So, no one messed with him.

Consequently, when I first joined his team, I stayed out of his way, like everyone else.

I did that for about four days.

That was when I decided to go against the advice of my colleagues. I decided that having an "arms length" relationship with this boss was simply asinine. So, I invited him to travel with me as we investigated some sticky employee relations issues at a few of our manufacturing locations, not knowing how he would respond.

He jumped at the chance.

I didn't necessarily need his help. But, I knew he loved manufacturing and getting out in the plants. As we traveled together, I used that time to get to know him better. As he talked about his family, kids, hobbies, education, previous jobs, our relationship warmed up significantly.

In the weeks that followed, though our conversations, I learned more about his personal operating style.

I learned about the subjects he was passionate about.

I learned the time he liked starting in the morning.

I learned when he liked to be deep in the details and when he preferred to be hands-off.

For example, because of his love of all things manufacturing, he wanted to get heavily involved in the labor relations stuff. However, he made it clear that he didn't care about the OD and team building initiatives we were working on and so he gave me lots of latitude on those initiatives.

I discovered how he liked to play corporate politics too. I took note of those situations when he didn't hesitate to throw his weight around with the higher ups to get what he wanted… as well as those instances when he would try to impress them, which wasn't too often.

I also discovered not to attempt reaching him at 10 AM or 2 PM. He would generally duck out to grab a smoke, a habit he had concealed from everyone but his executive assistant.

I used all this information and created a phenomenal relationship with him that exists to this day. In turn, he made lots of time for me on his schedule to share his prodigious experiences. I also got great reviews from him and he became one of my biggest advocates in the organization. It was one of the best work experiences I ever had.

Go First. Waiting for Your Boss to Reach Out
To You – Creates Success in Waiting, Not
In Building The Relationship

From this experience, I learned that no matter what you may initially think of your boss or what his or her reputation is, you have to own this relationship. That means, taking on sole responsibility for growing the relationship and being prepared to do all the heavy lifting. And that starts with going to school on your boss. You need to know your boss as a person, how he or she likes to operate, their likes, dislikes, preferences and style. And then like any good student, you use that info to adjust your approach to your HR work to meet his or her needs.

Here are some other strategies for successfully managing this critical relationship:

Keep your boss' agenda ahead of your own. If the boss wants you to drop everything you're working on and gather some turnover numbers for him, do it. If this means diverting your attention from something you consider a higher priority, don't complain. Just calmly explain that and let the boss decide the priority. Also, whatever his pace is throughout the day (fast moving or more deliberate), that should be yours too. If he likes bullet-pointed executive summaries, without all the detail, then that's what you should learn to like as well.

Learn the way your boss prefers to communicate and adapt. You can expect that it will be some mixture of one-on-ones, e-mail, phone, voicemail, or power point deck depending on what needs to be communicated and your boss' style. I've had bosses who prefer to keep 99% of all communications with me by e-mail and voicemail, rather than in-person. If that's the case, don't take it personally and try and change them...adapt. Even if he's a dominant electronic communicator, compensate for it by making it a point to set up regular face-to-face meetings: lunch, coffee, or quick 15 minute updates. It's the best way for you to maintain personal connections and to be sure you stay visible.

Establish an emotional bank account with your boss. To convert your boss into a career advocate or even potential godfather, it's important to treat him like a real person and make an authentic, emotional connection. Stephen Covey, in *The Seven Habits of Highly Effective People,* uses the metaphor of an emotional bank account to describe this. He talks about making "deposits" by proactively doing things that build trust in the relationship (like being honest, caring, kind and friendly)...or "withdrawals" by engaging in activities that decrease trust (like being unkind, disrespectful and insensitive). Obviously, you want to make more deposits and limit your withdrawals with your boss. In gradual ways, let him know who you really are... talk about your family, your spare time interests, movies, your cat, whatever. By connecting with him at a deep personal level, your relationship is like an emotional bank account. When you have wealth in your emotional bank account with him, the relationship is stable and can sustain disagreements or arguments, without killing your career. Conflicts with your boss can always be resolved. But when your account is low or even overdrawn, your relationship is in danger...and you need to be mindful to make deposits again, so it can be salvaged and survive.

If you're in your boss' doghouse or the relationship is headed south, start feeding your boss ideas and allow him to take the credit. This is a smart move for a number of reasons. One, no matter how much he brags about the new concept, in his mind he ultimately knows the real source – you. Plus, your chance of getting the idea implemented soars if your boss' owns it. And finally, it's a positive deposit in your emotional bank account with your boss and step towards rebuilding the relationship. Sure, you would like the credit, but many times that's not as important as getting something done and building great rapport with him.

Complement your boss. I'm not talking about brown nosing. I mean taking advantage of the differences between you and your boss. Sometimes, bosses hire you because you have strengths that compensate or augment his shortcomings. For example, I tend to be strategic on HR issues and not that detail-oriented. Simply put, in looking over the forest, sometimes I ignore the trees. Because of this blind spot, which I readily acknowledge, I tend to hire HR managers that are detail-oriented and terrific at follow-up. They complement me well. And, I've promoted many of them into bigger HR jobs because of this fact and because they were great performers.

Always be prepared for any discussions with your boss. Have your agenda, talking points and your point of view ready on your key projects. Sometimes these interactions are scheduled, sometimes impromptu. If the latter, be ready to think on your feet. Stick to a simple agenda, and try to control the conversation by being simple and direct. Follow up with a short e-mail summary of the next steps from the conversation as a little electronic paper trail of what went down, just in case.

Keep your boss up to speed on what you're doing. Most bosses hate surprises. A brief monthly update on your accomplishments (bullets only) will help him stay grooved on how you're progressing. I've never had a boss that has gotten annoyed at updates and are quite appreciative, especially if he has to update his boss on what's going on.

Dazzle your boss by over-delivering. Every time. By doing this, you control your boss' perception of you as a can-do winner versus someone who is just scraping by. Seize every chance to surprise him with an extra dash of excellence. This is your opportunity to make him look good and position yourself like an addictive drug that he simply can't resist.

NEVER contradict your boss in public. If you're looking for a quick one-way ticket to your boss' dog house, this is it. You only need to do it one time. That's right, just one slight slip of the tongue can send your career down in flames faster than you can say "outplacement." Are you wondering if this is just a scare tactic here or am I actually trying to tell you something? Well, you should know by now that I'm not above scare tactics, but this time I am trying to tell you something. And here is that something – in these situations, keep your trap shut!

If you're ever in a meeting and you boss is delivering incorrect information, *and his boss is in the room,* DO NOT CORRECT HIM. Even if he's totally wrong. Even if he's going to end up looking like a jerk for being wrong. Even if other people in the room realize he's wrong. Don't do it. Even if he tells you beforehand it's ok to do. Let someone else do the correcting. Let them be the one to "help" the boss.

As you might imagine, there is a story behind all these warnings. And you're right.

One time, at a meeting with the Pepsi senior leadership team, in response to a question, my boss rambled on and on about our unbelievable progress on diversity. He beamed with pride as he, off the top of his head, shared numbers to support our progress in retaining African-American, Latino and Asian females. Most of us on the team knew that the boss was quoting incorrect numbers and I sat back and watched puzzled glances being exchanged up and down the table.

My colleagues across the table and I were engaged in a wide-eyed mental telepathy exchange. We were thinking, "Oh my God he's doing it again." But none of us was going to stick our neck out and correct him. His mistake would be realized after the meeting and we'd point this out to him then...now now.

Anyway, we were all hoping he'd simply change the subject, but kept going on and on. Then, the new HR leader who just joined our team, Sharon, chimed in a very friendly and helpful tone: "Boss, I think the overall numbers you're referring to are only up 2% over last year, not 22%."

Well, you could have heard a pin drop in that room. All eyes turned to the boss. His face turned red and he somehow managed to finesse his way through the rest of the presentation by giving some lame excuse for his error. My well-meaning colleague looked on with complete fear, for she knew immediately that she had screwed up.

After the meeting ended, the boss informed Sharon that he wanted to see her in his office immediately. We never found out what was said behind those closed doors. And while Sharon didn't get fired, she was very clearly on the boss' blacklist for a very long time after that.

Let me be clear: challenging facts and pushing back frequently (even on your boss) is an important part of your career advancement repertoire. There is no better way to be authentic and gain credibility and respect as an HR professional...*but only if you do it at the right time.* And, doing it an open forum to your boss in front of his boss and other higher ups is <u>not</u> the right time.

If Sharon felt compelled to point out this mistake to the boss, as she should have, a better time would have been to approach him privately after the meeting was over. Lesson learned.

Unwritten HR Rule #21

No matter what his or her reputation is, take the initiative for building a great relationship with your boss. Waiting for the boss to reach out to you first creates success in waiting – not in building the relationship.

22

THE MOST IMPORTANT UNWRITTEN HR RULE OF ALL

A Special Bonus Secret!

Hopefully, you've enjoyed the first 21 secrets and you're now ready to put some of them into action.

However, my goal is to over-deliver in this book and make sure you get as much value as possible. So I've decided to include one more extra bonus secret – number 22. As you will see shortly, this chapter is a very personal one for me and painful to write in spots. But I believe that you will find this to be the most important chapter in this entire book and one you'll want to come back to and re-read periodically.

So, let's begin.

As HR professionals, we all want to make our mark. Deep down, we all want to be remembered and leave a legacy in the profession. It's human nature. For some people, it's being known as a great HR leader for their company. For others, it may be creating a leadership development program second to none that people rave about for years. Or for still others, it might be achieving recognition as the absolute best at talent acquisition, benefits administration, or labor relations.

These are all noble aspirations. But, I want to challenge you to shoot even higher. I want to encourage you to use the platform you have in HR to take your career to a level beyond these successes and use it to build a lasting legacy.

However, let me prepare you. Right now I could tell you how to do this in a couple of sentences or by jotting this down on a 3x5 card. But you wouldn't get the richness and the full power of this secret because *you have to understand the story behind it.* When I've shared this secret without the story, people react in weirdest and most unpredictable ways. Sometimes eyes glaze over. Other times, people switch topics. They almost always become uncomfortable. And they often say things like:

"Yeah, duh, ok....right."

"I'm not sure I get how that can drive the business forward."

"That's so motherhood and apple pie."

And, unfortunately, those reactions prevent them from understanding it's truly awesome power.

Having said all that, I'll concede that implementing this secret, while simple, is certainly not easy. Your biggest obstacle in applying it will *not* be your boss, your job, your peers, your spouse, or even your clients from hell. The biggest obstacle will be YOU. You will have to put aside what others may have told you about achieving HR success in order to make this one simple secret work for you.

I actually stumbled upon this early in my life. But like many people, I just quickly pushed it aside too. Sure, from time to time, I dabbled at it a bit. I did this more unconsciously than anything else, because I didn't really understand its real power. So I didn't get the maximum value from it.

And to be candid, I was too busy being busy. Working long hours. Climbing the corporate ladder. Making money. Trying to make a name for myself. Keeping up with the Joneses. Having fun. Trying to live large.

What I didn't recognize was that I was wasting lots of time. If I had started applying the principles behind this one simple secret sooner, I probably would have accomplished all the goals

I wound up achieving anyway – but would have accomplished them a lot faster and would have enjoyed it more.

But one incident really inspired me to get off my butt and start putting this little secret in motion. This one incident exposed me to its full force. Frankly, it smacked me right in the face. I have never forgotten it. And I never will.

Unfortunately, what finally got me going was a personal tragedy. Even more than that, it was the single most painful event I've ever experienced.

What was that incident?

It was the death of my son.

Life Is Pretty Easy Until Bad News
Knocks On Your Door

They say parents should never have to bury their children. And, in my wildest dreams, I never imagined that it would happen to me...with my only child. Those were things that happened to other people.

And I wasn't ready for it.

But, of course, no one ever is.

But it happened. And from that point forward, my life and HR career have never been the same.

It all started on January 8, at 3:30 AM. For some reason that night I was restless. I was just lying in bed with my eyes wide open. I didn't feel like reading. I didn't feel like sleeping. I was just staring at the ceiling daydreaming.

The phone rang. On the third ring, I reached for the phone and saw on caller ID that it was a call from Bryan's mom.

Getting a call at 3:30 AM, I immediately suspected the worse.

Unfortunately, the worse proved to be true.

Fighting through tears and barely able to talk, Bryan's mom managed to utter the words of my biggest nightmare:

Bryan had died in a car accident.

He was a few weeks short of his 25th birthday.

Bryan Collins was a student at Tennessee State University and was enrolled in the master's program in physical therapy.

161

Later, we learned that his overturned car was discovered by a rescue unit according to the Nashville Police report. The report went on to state that Bryan was "traveling north bound on Schrader Lane on the Tennessee State University campus when his vehicle ran off the left side of the road and hit a ditch."

After hanging up, in an instant, my life fell apart in ways I could never have fathomed. My mind went blank. I only remember staring in space, my vision blurred with tears, my heart racing as memories and pain flashed and flooded over me all at the same time. I could feel churning in my stomach and a throbbing throughout my body I could not have imagined was possible. I kept telling myself that this must be a dream. It all seemed so unreal.

The few days that followed took place in a fog. It was hard to concentrate on anything. I didn't eat. I couldn't sleep. I didn't feel like doing much. But there was work to be done. His mom and I had to plan Bryan's funeral. Thankfully, we had lots of help from our families. And while countless friends and relatives stopped by to offer their condolences, talk and help out, all I really wanted was to be alone with my thoughts.

Emotionally, I was a basket case. I was looking for someone to blame. And, I blamed everybody.

I blamed his mom. If she had just been more patient in our marriage, we would have never divorced. Things would have been different. And this would never have happened.

I blamed Bryan. All this would not have happened if he hadn't decided to return to TSU for graduate studies. He should have gone to another school. If he had done that, he'd still be living.

I blamed myself. I wasn't there as much as I needed to be. I was always in meetings, scrambling to meet deadlines, traveling or too busy with any number of HR projects. I should have called Bryan more. I should have visited him on campus more. I should have spent more time with him and less time at work. My priorities robbed us both of additional time we could have spent together.

And yes, I blamed God. I couldn't understand the wisdom of taking the innocent life of someone who hadn't harmed anyone and who had his entire life ahead of him.

Despite my internal rage and anger, which I'm sure Bryan's mom felt as well, we worked together with our families and devoted friends to prepare the funeral arrangements.

When the day of his funeral arrived we were ready. Everything was all set. Personally, I just wanted to get through the day.

We entered the black limo and were taken to the church.

However, When We Arrived, I Was Not Prepared For What We Saw

What I saw absolutely astounded me!

The parking lot was crowded. The line outside of church was so long you would have thought this was a sold out rock concert. When I got inside the church, all the pews in the church were packed. There were people standing who could not be seated. There was a fifty person choir. There were so many flowers there it felt like the botanical gardens. The funeral director told us that some of the flowers had to remain at the funeral home because there was no more room at the church for them.

This absolutely was the largest funeral I had ever attended.

Walking down the aisle of the church, I looked around I saw a lot of familiar faces. Friends and family. Colleagues from Pepsi and Quaker. I was very grateful and touched that many had traveled all the way from Chicago to Atlanta to attend the funeral to help us celebrate Bryan's life.

However, I saw many others there I didn't know. Some were there in suits, ties and dresses. And still others came in jeans and sweat shirts. From what I could tell, these were mostly college kids and grad students around Bryan's age. I also saw a few of the administrators and faculty from the university.

I didn't realize what was happening until Dr. John Cade, a dean at Tennessee State University, who we asked to speak on behalf of the school, came to microphone to deliver his remarks.

The first thing he did was to ask all the students, administrators and faculty of the university to stand.

It seemed like half of the church stood up. He told us that many had driven over four hours from Nashville to Atlanta to attend the funeral.

But that wasn't all.

The following week, the university held its own special memorial service for Bryan. I was surprised again, as more than 300 students, administrators, faculty, and parents packed themselves into the Thomas E. Poag Auditorium on campus to reminisce about Bryan and the impact he had on their lives. Ironically, the campus memorial service occurred on Monday, January 23 on what would have been Bryan's 25th birthday.

Before the memorial service began, many of the students approached Bryan's mom and me to apologize for not being able to travel the prior week to Atlanta for the funeral. As we continued to meet and greet students, I mentally calculated that there were close to 700 people combined who attended the two services,

As all this was going on, there was one question that I couldn't quite figure out and that was...

Why did all these people come?

Well, I soon learned the answer very quickly. At the campus memorial services, one by one, students stood up and shared stories about how Bryan had helped, supported or touched them in some way.

William Busch, my son's fraternity brother and close friend, shared the times they spent together and one valuable lesson that my son gave him: "Bryan taught me how to be selfless."

Clifton Gray, another fraternity brother, stood up and told the audience: "He carried our fraternity and was the glue that held us together. He gave us encouragement and that truly influenced everyone...and he will always be remembered in our hearts forever."

Jarrod Uddin, who was the reigning Mr. Tennessee State University, talked about how Bryan helped him win the contest.

"Bryan came in second place in the Mr. TSU contest the year before and lost by only one vote. He could have been jealous and bitter. Instead, he supported and encouraged me. Before I went on stage to compete in the contest, I was by myself and nervous. When Bryan saw how jittery and uncertain I was, he walked over and put his hand on my shoulder and smiled. He then gave me some words of encouragement, led me in a little private prayer and told me to go out there and win. And I did."

Scores of students, faculty and strangers relayed similar experiences and memorable situations about some way Bryan had influenced them.

Listening to these stories, I realized then why all these people gathered.

They weren't there because Bryan was some famous local politician. Or some celebrity superstar. Or even some prominent, well-paid HR executive.

They Were There To Pay Tribute To Someone Who Had Brought Joy Into Their Lives.

As I listened to the stories, I heard some common themes. For example:

Sometimes he gave a kind word at just the right time.
Sometimes he listened when no one else would.
Sometimes he gave encouragement.
Sometimes he gave only a simple smile.
Sometimes he went out of his way to do a special favor.
Sometimes he gave nothing more than an open mind.
Sometimes he gave his time, when he could have chosen not to.
Sometimes he was helping others believe in themselves.
Sometimes he was giving tough love when nobody would.
Sometimes he was simply being a friend at a time of need.

This was the reason so many people showed up. And, at that moment a father couldn't be prouder of his son than I was of mine.

I then thought about me. My own mortality. My own life. My HR career. And that's when it hit me!

When you're gone...

- Someone else takes that HR VP job you had and you will be quickly forgotten...except by the people who will remember the joy you brought into their lives when you freely gave them your time and advice when they were stuck deciding how to best advance in their own HR career.
- Someone else stays up all night to prepare that HR strategy presentation for the leadership team and nobody will remember it or you...except for those people on your team who remember the joy your brought into their lives when you took time to publicly recognize their efforts in helping you pull that presentation together.
- As the years pass, no one will remember that it was you who negotiated that landmark, innovative labor union contract and you could feel unappreciated...except by the scores of HR folks that were grateful for the time you drew upon this experience to personally coach them on their own labor contract negotiations.

Yes, when you're gone...

All The Valuable Experiences, Life Lessons and Skills You Gained In Your HR Career Die With You....Unless You Figure Out A Way To Use Them To Truly Benefit Others And Bring Joy Into Their Lives.

The Only REAL Successes You Have As An HR Professional That Will Be Remembered Will Be Those That Live On In The Hearts, Minds and Memories Of The People You Help Along The Way.

I got the message. And, in that instant, I re-purposed my life. I decided to begin spending more of my personal time, talents, and resources towards making a difference and bringing more joy into the lives of other people. As a first step, I started the Bryan A. Collins Memorial Scholarship program at Tennessee State University. It became then and is now my vehicle for keeping Bryan's memory alive and for bringing joy into the lives of high potential, minority students who need financial assistance to achieve their dream of become college graduates. Separately, I decided to start SuccessInHR.com, write this book and develop other ways of sharing my knowledge and giving back to the HR profession. All of this was and has been inspired by Bryan.

And That, My Friend, Is The Challenge I'd Like To Give You As An HR Professional

While you're taking time to advance your HR career, I'd also like to encourage you to ALSO FIND TIME to give back, bring joy or make a difference in the lives of others.

Don't misunderstand. I am not suggesting that there is anything wrong with having career goals, aggressively pursuing success, building wealth and helping your organization succeed. That's what this book is all about, right?

However, I am encouraging you to use the terrific platform you have as an HR professional to ALSO make a difference. Life is short. Your HR career is even shorter. You never know when either might end.

Helping other people and organizations is the heart of the HR profession. You, like me, were probably drawn to the field for this reason. So in HR you have a natural platform to assist and enable others. One very successful senior executive at Frito-Lay who I worked with at Pepsi, calls this "servant leadership" and asks himself at the end of each day how helpful he's been with each person he's seen that day and then how he can be more helpful tomorrow. When tomorrow comes, he goes through the same process again.

There Are Endless Ways To Give Back, Bring Joy
And Make A Lasting Difference With Others

The key is to change your focus from "me" to "you" and set aside time to do this. This simple shift in your mindset and focus can single-handedly turn around your HR career all by itself. But you must build time into your calendar and look for ways to put your needs second to those of your team, your boss, your clients or others that you care about. This could include things like:

- Volunteering to coach or mentor those with less HR experience.
- Taking time to personally step in and help onboard new people in your organization who are scared and feel abandoned in their first few weeks on the job.
- Putting yourself in someone's life as a sounding board when they are struggling to succeed on the job.
- Seeking out those who are doing a great job, but are going unrecognized for their efforts. Administrative assistants, technicians or other back office employees are great examples of those doing terrific work but whose efforts often go unappreciated.
- Letting a high school student or college intern "shadow" you for a day to observe you on the job.
- Sharing your HR story or experience on campuses, at Career Days and with HR associations.
- Introducing people in your network to others or helping to connect people together.
- Sharing your HR experiences in a book, blog, white paper or posting it online for the entire world of HR to benefit from.
- Volunteering at your local Boys and Girls Club.
- Contributing your time to advancing causes that you are passionate about.
- Just showing everyday kindness.

To further illustrate, let's take the first example above. No matter who you are or what you've done, there is almost always someone more junior, just a few steps behind you who can learn from your HR examples and experiences. You are a role model to them. And the help you could provide, at just the right moment when they felt down and depressed, could have a tremendous long-term impact on the rest of their career.

And this person will keep your legacy alive forever.

When you do this, something else amazing will happen. It's called the boomerang effect. Or as it's better known... the "what goes around comes around" effect.

Like me, you've probably heard this saying referred to all your life. While I knew what it meant, I never experienced it in any meaningful way until I started stepping up my efforts to be of more service to others. And I've found out that it's true. I've learned that people ARE more willing follow you, cooperate with you, and support your ideas when you put their interests first. It's this boomerang effect in action.

So What Is It That You Want Most To "Boomerang" Back Into Your HR Career Right Now? Whatever It Is, Use The Boomerang Effect To Help You Go Get It

* Want better relationships with your HR colleagues?
- Then, go help a friend or HR colleague improve their professional relationships.

* Want to feel good about yourself?
- Then, go give someone else a lift and help them feel better about themselves.

* Want to have more fun at work?
- Then, make work more interesting and fun for your team and the people around you.

* Want to be inspired?
- Then, go and inspire someone else...your team, your colleagues, your kids.

* Want some help with your job search or career?
- Then, go help someone who needs help with looking for a new job.

* Want more time?
- Then, give some of your time to others.
- Share some HR time management tips with someone else.

* Want more contacts?
- Then, connect others to people in your network.

* Want to do more meaningful HR work?
- Then, help someone else find meaning in their work.

* Want a better boss?
- Then, start being a better leader to your own team. If you don't lead an HR team, become a better leader to your clients, your community, or your colleagues?

* Want to be valued and respected?
- Then, start valuing and respecting others more.
- Better still, start valuing and respecting yourself more and others will follow.

* Want more money?
- Then, give what you can by means of a donation or assistance to someone else.

* Want better career opportunities?
- Then, help create opportunities for others.

When You Do This, A Few Things Happen:

You will immediately feel good about yourself. Giving and helping others will give you a natural high which helps you move towards your own goals. Sometimes your efforts are noticed and appreciated; other times they are not. None of that matters. All that matters is that YOU know and that you get the positive feelings that result.

You strengthen your relationships with the people you've helped and you become a lot more influential with other people. Stronger relationships make you much stronger and a lot more effective in your HR career.

You will see the thing that you gave away starting to show up...just like a boomerang...but very often from a completely different direction, or in a completely different way than you ever expected...and on its own schedule, not yours.

All of this may seem completely counter-intuitive to give away that which you want most - but I've found that it works for me. Why don't you try this and see if it will work for you? However, don't over-think, over-analyze, or over-rationalize this, just give it a shot. If it doesn't work for you, you can always drop it.

But I predict that it will work...and that you'll find that the most gratifying moments in your career will occur when you begin to utilize your HR position as a vehicle for making a difference and bringing joy to other people.

And that, my friend, is what attaining awesome success in HR is all about.

Onward!

Unwritten HR Rule #22

**The Most Important Unwritten
HR Rule Of All**

*All the valuable experiences, life lessons and skills
you gained in your HR career die with you…
unless you figure out a way to use them
to truly benefit others, make a difference
and bring joy into their lives.*

*The only REAL successes you have as an HR pro-
fessional that will be remembered will be those
that live on in the hearts, minds and
memories of the people you help
along the way.*

*"A candle's flame can live forever, if it is
used to light enough other candles."*

*"Don't chase success. Put together an HR
career that truly inspires and helps other
people succeed and success
will chase you."*

A FINAL WORD
LOOKING FORWARD

Thank you for reading *Unwritten HR Rules*. It is my sincere hope that you were able to extract a few nuggets of wisdom that you can put into action right away. As we wrap up, there are a few final words I'd like to leave you with.

This is an extraordinary time to be an HR professional.

Despite the economy, the future is bright for the entire Human Resources field. Obviously I'm biased, but I've never met a CEO not interested in improving the performance of their business through people. And working with business leaders throughout your organization in crafting initiatives that can do this is exactly what HR is all about. This will not change. So, despite what you've read, HR is not going to disappear anytime soon.

To this end, as I look into my crystal ball, there are a variety of challenges and opportunities on the horizon you should prepare yourself for:

Most large businesses are going global or have already, so the HR executive of the future will absolutely need to have international experience and be able to design HR strategies that can fit the cultures of India, China, Germany and other countries in Asia and Western Europe.

As more baby boomers defer retirements because of the recession, the HR leader will need to help address generational issues at work. We'll see more innovations in benefits like elder care, pet care, concierge services, paid time off and flextime. With companies competing for top talent, HR folks will need to come up with these and other creative benefit programs to meet the diverse generational needs of the millennials, the Generation Xs and Ys they want to attract and keep.

Technology innovations will continue to be big. Enterprise-wide platforms like SAP and PeopleSoft (and their successors) that simplify and standardize HR transactions will continue to evolve. So will the use of social networks in recruiting and the use of virtual teams of employees who communicate through video-conferencing, e-mail, text messaging and Twitter. Online technologies that allow more work to be done without much face-to-face interaction will also grow by leaps and bounds in the future. And, as an HR leader, you'll need to stay on the leading edge of all of this -- both for your department's own use and to ensure that people issues are being considered as your organization makes these types of technology investment decisions.

I believe we'll also see, as a result of the financial banking crisis, HR stepping up and playing a stronger internal role in the regulation of issues such as fairness in the workplace, executive pay, 401k's and ethics. Or at least, I hope so. No one wants their company to become the next AIG or go belly up.

I also look forward to the day that we won't have to have discussions about diversity and inclusion -- that it will be a natural part of how we do business. We should all work *every day* with our organizations to help us strive towards that ideal.

Finally, in the future, I'm confident we will see a career HR professional appointed as CEO of a Fortune 500 company. I don't know when it'll happen, but certainly it will happen in my lifetime. HR executives have already moved into senior-level positions in operations, marketing and sales for years with great success. So I believe it's only a matter of time. When that does happen, it'll be a great sign that the HR profession has finally arrived...and, who knows this first-ever CEO could be YOU!

Again, I hope these perspectives are encouraging and that you've enjoyed and profited from your investment in *Unwritten HR Rules*. I wish you much success in the future.

Best,
Alan

SUMMARY LIST OF UNWRITTEN HR RULES

No BS, Kick-Butt Secrets You Can't Count On Your Boss To Tell You About

Unwritten HR Rule #1:
You don't get promoted in HR, unless you promote yourself. Great ability is not enough, you also need great visibility.

Unwritten HR Rule #2
Embrace and use the F-word regularly. Set up regular face-to-face meetings to clarify, dig deeper and de-code any fuzzy feedback you receive. Consider feedback a gift and when receiving it, the most appropriate response is: "Thank you!"

Unwritten HR Rule #3
It's easy to impress your business leaders as an HR professional…when you've impressed them with your knowledge of their business first!

Unwritten HR Rule #3
The key to making a lot more money in HR is by adding massive value. Adding value is figuring out ways to improve results in areas your organization cares deeply about. And then doing it!

Unwritten HR Rule #5
Go small to grow big. Don't be afraid to specialize and niche yourself in HR. Go where your passion calls out to you, but make sure your HR specialty is valued by your organization or by other companies. If you absolutely must become a jack of all trades, then also become a master of ONE.

Unwritten HR Rule #6
To give yourself an edge as a serious contender for the bigger and broader HR roles (and to avoid the ax during tough periods),

you need to establish a consistent track record of acing perfor-mance reviews. And to do this, you must: document and do self-appraisals consistently, check in with your boss regularly, show clear business impact, quantify your contributions, and make sure you have at least one BIPP (a Bold Innovative Power Project) that clearly differentiates you from the HR pack.

Unwritten HR Rule #7
When you mess up, fess up. Fast!

Unwritten HR Rule #8
It's important that you look good online. Take 5 minutes per week to check Google, Facebook, and Twitter to protect your online HR image. Use ezinearticles.com to broaden your online exposure and reputation. Set up a Google alert for your name.

Unwritten HR Rule #9
Optimize your use of LinkedIn. As an HR professional, it's the best online tool you can use to keep your resume up to date, stay in touch with your network, search for jobs, prepare for inter-views and market yourself.

How To Make The Best HR Career Opportunities Come To You

Unwritten HR Rule #10
Follow the P.O.W.E.R. formula to tap into the hidden job market and make the best HR jobs come to you. This formula involves:
(1) Public Speaking in your HR area of expertise.
(2) Organization Leadership, not waiting on direction.
(3) Writing proactively online and offline.
(4) Everyday Meetings to enhance your impact.
(5) Representing Your Company and volunteering.

Unwritten HR Rule #11
Speaking and giving presentations in your HR area of expertise is one of the fastest ways to attract favorable attention from

those who can help advance your human resources career. Speaking gives you tremendous visibility and credibility by giving you an avenue to put your confidence, your mastery of an HR topic and your communications skills on display.

Unwritten HR Rule #12
There are HR leadership voids practically everywhere if you look for them. Stepping into these situations and taking charge is a great way of setting yourself apart from the rest of the HR pack.

Unwritten HR Rule #13
Writing is a powerful way to help others discover you. No matter how much (or how little) experience you have, the way your words come across on paper or electronically carries your name and reputation to people who might never learn of you otherwise.

Unwritten HR Rule #14
Showing up big and regularly contributing your ideas during everyday meetings is a great way to get noticed and labels you as a strong leader and someone capable of assuming broader HR accountabilities.

Unwritten HR Rule #15
Representing your company at external affairs, conferences or meetings is a great way to raise your professional profile and provide an avenue for HR job opportunities to come to you.

Engaging Other People To Help You Advance Your HR Career

Unwritten HR Rule #16
Lone rangers don't travel far up the HR ladder of success. You need to have a support system consisting of a G.R.A.N.D. circle of relationships. These include:
- A Godfather

- <u>R</u>eally Good Headhunters
- <u>A</u>dvisors and Mentors
- Your <u>N</u>etwork
- <u>D</u>irect Boss

Unwritten HR Rule #17
Having a godfather is crucial to your HR career. Godfathers are people who believe in you, act as your advocate and sponsor at the senior levels of the organization when key career decisions about you are being made. Unlike mentors, you cannot choose a godfather, they choose you.

Unwritten HR Rule #18
You should always have two good headhunters on speed dial. They are an important part of your Plan B strategy, should you find yourself suddenly in the job market.

Unwritten HR Rule #19
Don't hesitate to fully utilize advisors and mentors to take your HR career to the next level. Attract the ones you want by keeping the relationship informal, taking good care of it and by looking for ways to help them succeed.

Unwritten HR Rule #20
Network, network, network! Never stop nurturing or expanding your personal and professional connections.

Unwritten HR Rule #21
No matter what his or her reputation is, take the initiative for building a great relationship with your boss. Waiting for the boss to reach out to you first creates success in waiting – not in building the relationship.

Unwritten HR Rule #22
The Most Important Unwritten HR Rule Of All is…

ATTAINING AWESOME CAREER SUCCESS IN HR

All the valuable experiences, life lessons and skills you gained in your HR career die with you…unless you figure out a way to use them to truly benefit others, make a difference and bring joy into their lives.

The only REAL successes you have as an HR professional that will be remembered will be those that live on in the hearts, minds and memories of the people you help along the way.

###

THE BRYAN A. COLLINS SCHOLARSHIP PROGRAM

The Bryan A. Collins Memorial Scholarship Program awards scholarship grants every year to minority students who demonstrate excellence in pursuit of their college degrees. Students selected for this scholarship must embody the values embraced by the late Bryan A. Collins -- great with people, great at aca-academics and great in extra-curricular leadership activities.

Bryan Collins was a rising star and well-respected student leader at Tennessee State University. Bryan received his B.S. degree in Biology from TSU in May 2005. At the time of his passing, he was enrolled in the Masters program in physical therapy and anxiously looking forward to commencing his doctoral studies. On campus, he was a leader in the Kappa Alpha Psi fraternity, served on the Civic Committee, the Community Service Committee and help set strategic direction as a Board Member of the fraternity.

In addition, he found much success outside the classroom. He was voted Mr. Tennessee State first runner-up, was involved in the Student Union Board of Governors, was a founding member of the Generation of Educated Men and worked closely with the Tennessee State University dean of admissions and records.

Bryan found comfort and relaxation in sports, music, movies, video games, friends, good parties and just spending time with his family relaxing at home.

The key contributors to Bryan's scholarship program include the PepsiCo Foundation, Pamela Hewitt & Warren Lawson of Chicago, the Motorola Foundation and many other organizations and individuals. Additional details about Bryan, the scholarship program and how to contribute can be found at the scholarship website at: www.BryanCollinsScholarship.org.

ABOUT THE AUTHOR

Alan Collins is Founder of Success in HR, a company dedicated to empowering HR professionals and executives around the globe with insights and tools for enhancing their careers. He was formerly Vice President of Human Resources at Pepsi where he led HR initiatives for their North American Quaker Oats, Gatorade and Tropicana businesses.

With 25 years as an HR executive and professional, Alan's corporate and operating human resources experience is extensive. He led an organization of 60 HR directors, managers and professionals spread across 21 different locations in North America, where he was accountable for their performance, careers and success. He and his team provided HR strategic and executional oversight for a workforce of over 7000 employees supporting $8 billion in sales. Alan also served as the HR M&A lead in integrating new acquisitions as well as divesting existing businesses; and he provided HR leadership for one of the largest change initiatives in the history of the Pepsi organization.

Alan is also author of the *"Best Kept HR Secrets: 400 Powerful Tips for Thriving at Work, Making Yourself Indispensable & Attaining Outrageous Success in Human Resources"* and he has written over 100 articles and white papers on HR. His perspectives are regularly featured in various human resources publications, blogs and ezines worldwide.

Finally, Alan was selected as a member of the prestigious <u>Executive Leadership Council,</u> based in Washington D.C. In addition, he has also taught at various Chicago-area universities.

He received his BS and MS degrees in Industrial Relations from Purdue. More about Alan and his works can be accessed at: <u>www.SuccessInHR.com.</u>

Made in the USA
Lexington, KY
29 August 2011